*L*UNCHES *and* SUPPERS
with Schmecks Appeal

EDNA STAEBLER

McGraw-Hill Ryerson
Toronto   Montreal

McClelland & Stewart
Toronto

First published in 1991 by

MCGRAW-HILL RYERSON LIMITED
300 Water Street
Whitby, Canada
L1N 9B6

MCCLELLAND & STEWART LIMITED
481 University Avenue
Suite 900
Toronto, Canada
M5G 2E9

1 2 3 4 5 6 7 8 9 0 W 0 9 8 7 6 5 4 3 2 1

Canadian Cataloguing in Publication Data

Staebler, Edna, date
    Lunches and suppers with schmecks appeal

(Schmecks appeal cookbook series)
ISBN 0-7710-8272-X

1. Lunches.   2. Suppers.   3. Cookery, Mennonite.
4. Cookery — Ontario — Waterloo (Regional municipality).
I. Title.   II. Series: Staebler, Edna, date. The
Schmecks appeal cookbook series.

TX735.S85 1991   641.5'3   C90-095545-7

Printed and bound in Canada

This book was manufactured using acid-free paper.

CONTENTS

PLANNING A MEAL

One of the girls in our gang at high school was flirty, pretty, and bound to get a husband. She scoffed at those of us who were studying to go to university. When we left for Toronto, she went to Guelph to take the Wedding Ring Course at Macdonald Hall. As soon as she finished, she married a lawyer whose father built them a big, gabled house where she entertained elegantly with the help of her mother-in-law's maid.

Every Friday morning she sat down, as she'd been taught at Mac Hall, and made out menus for every day of the week to come. And she stuck to those menus. I don't know what she did when her husband called and said he couldn't make it home for lunch on Wednesday, or he was bringing a client home for dinner on Thursday, or if one of their children was invited to stay with a friend for supper and she had food left over. I often wondered what she did in emergencies but I never asked her.

She gained a reputation for being a great cook and hostess, and was very proud of herself. When anyone asked her for a recipe, she always said her recipes were her secret and she wouldn't give them to anyone.

I once had a neighbour whose husband died soon after she had her third baby; she took a course at business college, got a job, and paid a girl to look after the children till she came home at five. She planned all her meals ahead; she had to. She loved trying new recipes. When she invited friends for dinner, she'd know a week in advance what she'd give them to eat and she'd start preparing; her time was limited and scheduled.

When she retired and lived alone — with all her time for herself — she often had friends in for dinner and still planned and started days ahead to prepare a really classy repast with all the elaborate trimmings.

My sister Norma invites twelve to eighteen people for a buffet supper — then she's committed. She decides what she'll give them to eat and sticks to her decision, no

1

changing her mind, no saying, "Well, maybe I'll have this instead of that." She buys what she needs, makes what she can in advance, and at the last minute never seems flustered or hurried. She always turns out a meal that everyone raves about, and her guests always ask for, and are given, her recipes.

That's the way to do it. I know it works. Planning and preparing ahead are the way to enjoy entertaining.

I wish I would do it that way instead of the haphazard, rushed-at-the-last-minute method that is my habit. The result is that I avoid having parties. I don't invite people to come weeks ahead because it makes me nervous; with that much advance notice I have no excuse for not giving them the fabulous meal they expect from the author of a cookbook.

I like to call my friends at noon to come for supper that night; I tell them not to expect a production, just an unfancy, lazy meal. When someone visits me for a week or a weekend, I run to the market, fill up my fridge with whatever is fresh in the season, and feel confident that no one will starve. All I have to do is make something out of what's there.

It's a poor system. It is no system. I don't recommend it. But my friends keep coming back; some even help me prepare whatever I have. Our joy is in eating and being together.

CASSEROLES AND ONE-DISH MEALS

EVA'S ASPARAGUS CASSEROLE

This can be expanded or made as small as you like — a perfect meal by itself.

Noodles, cooked
Raw asparagus
Seasonings
Ground beef (optional)
Cheese sauce (page 88)
Grated cheese and breadcrumbs

Eva says, "Put noodles in the bottom of a buttered casserole, then put in as much asparagus as you need; over the asparagus spread a layer of ground beef, seasoned with salt and pepper; make a cheese sauce and pour it over — enough so you'll have plenty of moisture. Spread grated cheese mixed with breadcrumbs on top and bake in a 350°F oven for 45 minutes or an hour, depending on how large a batch you make."

ASPARAGUS AND EGG CASSEROLE

A great luncheon dish with hot biscuits.

2 slices buttered bread broken into crumbs
1 pound fresh cooked asparagus,
cut in 1-inch pieces
4 hardcooked eggs, sliced
4 tablespoons butter
2 tablespoons flour
½ teaspoon salt
1 cup milk
1 cup Cheddar cheese, diced

Put half the buttered crumbs in a buttered baking dish; spread the cooked asparagus pieces over the crumbs and the egg slices over the asparagus. Blend 2 tablespoons of the butter, the flour, salt, and milk with the cheese and pour over all. Top with the remaining breadcrumbs mixed with the remaining 2 tablespoons melted butter. Bake at 350°F for 30 minutes.

3

CHICKEN AND ASPARAGUS CASSEROLE

Here's one for the asparagus season. If you can't wait for spring, you could use canned or frozen asparagus.

3 tablespoons butter
3 tablespoons flour
1 cup milk
1 cup chicken broth
½ cup mayonnaise
1 teaspoon lemon juice
Salt
1 pound asparagus
2 cups cooked chicken pieces

Melt butter. Blend in the flour, milk, and chicken broth, stirring until thick and smooth. Away from heat stir in the mayonnaise, lemon juice, and salt. Arrange asparagus — whole or in pieces — in a baking dish. Place the chicken on top and pour the sauce over all. Bake in a 375°F oven for 30 minutes or just long enough to cook the asparagus. If you use canned asparagus, it takes only 20 minutes.

NORM'S CHICKEN AND POTATO CHIP CASSEROLE

This is easy to prepare and makes a big hit at a supper party.

1 or 2 chickens, cut into pieces
1 pound mushrooms, sliced
2 tablespoons butter
2 or 3 long stalks celery, cut up
1 can mushroom soup, mixed with
1 can milk
Several cups potato chips, crumbled
1 cup slivered almonds

Boil chicken pieces until tender. Sauté mushrooms in butter, then mix with celery and mushroom soup blended with milk. Into a greased casserole, put a layer of the cooked chicken pieces, cover them with a layer of crumbled potato chips, sprinkle on some of the almonds, then add some of the mushroom mixture. Repeat until you've filled the dish and used all the ingredients, with chips and almonds on top. Bake at 350°F for about 40 minutes. Serve with a hot vegetable, jellied or green salad, cranberry sauce or apple halves, and hot rolls.

CHICKEN À LA KING

When we were teenagers, a party wasn't a party unless we were served Chicken à la King. The girls always had two, the boys three. We were all skinny in those days.

2 tablespoons butter
½ cup flour
3½ cups chicken stock
3 cups diced cooked chicken
1 cup chopped mushrooms, cooked in butter
Salt and pepper
1 cup green peas, cooked
2 egg yolks, beaten
¾ cup whole milk or cream
⅓ cup pimiento, chopped (for colour)
12 flaky pastry patty shells

Melt the butter, add the flour, blend, then stir in the chicken stock and cook until thickened. Add the chicken, mushrooms, seasonings, and peas. Beat the egg yolks, stir in the milk or cream and blend with the chicken mixture over low heat until it is smooth and thick. Before serving, stir in the pimiento. Fill the patty shells generously, with some filling flowing over on the plate. A salad and rolls alongside and we were a happy gang.

STUFFED ZUCCHINI

The zucchinis in Barbie's garden hide under the leaves and almost overnight seem to grow to the size of canoes. This is a good way to use one. You don't have to follow the recipe exactly but it will give you the general drift.

> 1 huge zucchini, or several smaller ones
> ¼ cup oil
> ½ cup finely chopped onion
> ½ teaspoon finely chopped garlic
> ½ pound ground beef
> 1 egg, lightly beaten
> ¼ cup ham, or bacon (or skip it)
> ½ cup fresh breadcrumbs
> 6 tablespoons Parmesan cheese or other
> ½ teaspoon oregano
> ½ teaspoon salt, or more
> ¼ teaspoon black pepper
> 2 cups tomato sauce or soup (optional)

Cut zucchini in half lengthwise and spoon out most of the pulp leaving the boatlike shell. Chop pulp coarsely. Heat oil in a frying pan, add onions and cook until soft. Add zucchini pulp and garlic, cook 4 minutes, stirring often. Spoon this into a large sieve and set over a bowl to let drain. Heat 1 tablespoon oil in the pan, add ground beef and brown, stirring with a fork to break lumps. Drain the beef of fat. Combine vegetables and beef, beat in the egg, ham, breadcrumbs, 2 tablespoons Parmesan, oregano, salt, and pepper. Spoon into zucchini boats, mounding slightly on top. Sprinkle top with remaining 4 tablespoons cheese. Place the zucchini in a baking dish, pour the tomato sauce around it, cover it with foil if the dish doesn't have a lid. Bake at 375°F for 30 minutes. Ten minutes before serving, remove foil so the top will brown.

ZUCCHINI CASSEROLE

This is a godsend during the zucchini season; it should generously serve eight but six will finish it.

1½ pounds zucchini
2 tablespoons butter
1 cup grated onion
1 clove garlic, finely chopped
1 pound ground beef
1 ½ cups cooked rice
1 teaspoon basil
2 cups cottage cheese
3 or 4 tomatoes, cut in pieces
⅔ cup water
1 cup grated Cheddar cheese

Cut zucchini into ¼-inch slices. Put one-half into a buttered casserole. Melt the butter. Add onion and garlic, and cook until onions are transparent but not brown. Stir in the beef and cook until lightly browned, then add the rice and basil. Spoon the beef mixture over the zucchini in the casserole. Cover with the cottage cheese and remaining zucchini. Spread the tomato pieces over all. Pour in water. Sprinkle grated cheese over top and bake at 350°F for 1 hour, or until the zucchini is tender.

BAKED STUFFED PEPPER SQUASH

You can make a complete meal of this with a light salad.

Wash the **squash**, cut it in half, scoop out the seeds and place the halves cut-side down in a pan. Pour ¼-inch of water around the squash and bake at 400°F for half an hour. Now turn the squash cut-side up and fill the hollows with partially cooked **sausage meat**. (You can form the sausage into patties and put them in the oven when you first put the squash in.) Bake until tender — about half an hour.

Or you can stuff the squash with a rich **bread dressing** and serve your meat separately.

Or you can combine a **bread dressing** with **ground beef or sausage** meat and bake in the squash, as in Stuffed Zucchini.

EMERGENCY CASSEROLE

You can easily stretch this casserole if Uncle George and Aunt Mimi drop in and obviously expect to be invited for lunch or supper.

> **1 or 2 onions, chopped**
> **2 stalks celery, chopped**
> **½ to 1 green pepper, fresh or frozen, chopped**
> **(optional)**
> **2 to 4 tablespoons butter**
> **3 to 4 cups vegetable, V8, or tomato juice**
> **½ package noodles**
> **1 teaspoon dried basil (optional)**
> **3 to 6 wieners, sliced ⅛ inch thick**
> **1 cup grated cheese**

In a heavy pot with a lid, sauté the onion, celery, and pepper in the butter for about 7 minutes. Stir in the juice, noodles and basil, cover and cook over medium heat, stirring fairly often until the noodles are tender. Stir in the wiener slices. Sprinkle the grated cheese over the top, and cover until the cheese is melted. Or — what I do — scrape the noodle mixture into a casserole dish, sprinkle the cheese on top, and put the dish in a 300°F oven or under the broiler until the cheese is melted and you and yours are ready to eat it.

CASSEROLE FOR CAROL AND PAUL

Some of the most surprisingly good dishes are made of leftovers. In late August I impulsively invited a young couple for dinner. I had some cooked green beans left from my Sunday dinner and four cooked cobs of corn, tomatoes, onions, and a piece of pork sausage frozen in my fridge. Enough for a casserole, I decided.

I cut the **corn** from the cobs, sliced up a couple of **onions**, added the **green beans**, enough cut-up **tomatoes** to give plenty of moisture, and **salt, pepper**, and **parsley**. I boiled and browned the **sausage** before cutting it up into bite-sized pieces and mixing it with the vegetables in a buttered casserole. (I might have used cut-up wieners.) I covered it all with a thick layer of **grated cheese** mixed with **corn flakes**, put it in the oven at 350°F for about half an hour — till the top was crusty and golden — then served it with hot buns and a salad. Those kids ate every bit of what looked like enough for five or six people.

WIENER-VEGETABLE CASSEROLE

This is one of those handy-dandy one-dish recipes that can be contracted or expanded and substituted to suit your needs. If you keep a package of frankfurters and peas frozen in your fridge, it's perfect for an emergency — or otherwise.

> **3 cups sliced potatoes**
> **2 tablespoons flour**
> **1 teaspoon salt**
> **Pepper**
> **1 cup sliced carrots**
> **1 or 2 onions, sliced**
> **½ cup cut-up celery tops or stalks**
> **2 tablespoons cut-up parsley**
> **1½ cups milk**
> **6, 8, 10 or more frankfurters**
> **Bacon slices to cover**

Grease a casserole — or a deep flat baking dish with a lid if you want more surface. Spread half the potatoes in the bottom, sprinkle with flour, salt, and pepper; arrange the other vegetables over the potatoes, sprinkle them the same way, then put the rest of the potatoes over the top. Pour milk over all — enough to almost cover, but not too close to the top of the dish. Arrange wieners on top and bacon slices covering the wieners. Cover and cook at 375°F for 50 minutes. Uncover for 10 minutes to crisp the bacon. The wieners will be puffy and brown when you take them out of the stove; they shrink unless you gobble them quickly.

ONE-DISH BARBECUE FRANKS

Lorna told me that not only kids love this flavourful frank-furter casserole.

10 small potatoes, unpeeled
3 tablespoons melted butter, margarine, or oil
¼ cup coarsely chopped onions
1 tablespoon butter or vegetable oil
½ cup water
½ cup ketchup
¼ cup lemon juice
4 teaspoons sugar
4 teaspoons Worcestershire sauce
1 teaspoon dry mustard
1 package frankfurters

Cook the potatoes in 1 inch of boiling salted water, covered, for 15 minutes. Drain and place in a large baking dish; brush with melted butter. Brown in 450°F oven, turning once. Meanwhile in a small skillet, sauté onion in butter, add remaining ingredients except franks. Bring to a boil. Slit the frankfurters. Turn oven to 350°F and arrange franks over the potatoes in the baking dish; pour the sauce over them. Bake 20 minutes, basting and turning once.

BEVVY'S ALLES TZSAMMA
(All Together in One Dish)

You could hide a few leftovers in this, too, if you wished.

Slice a layer of **raw, peeled potatoes** into the bottom of a buttered casserole; then a layer of **sliced onions**, **green beans or peas** (or both), a layer of **ground beef**, slices of **green pepper** and, topping all, a thick layer of fresh **tomatoes** (or canned) to give moisture to the dish. Sprinkle **salt** and **pepper** over the various layers. Bake in a 300°F oven for about an hour. And there's your nourishing, tasty meal — with a lettuce salad.

KRAUT WICKEL
(Cabbage Rolls)

This Oktoberfest dish can be made with variations.

1 cup rice
Consommé or beef broth
10 to 12 outer cabbage leaves
1 pound ground beef (raw or cooked)
1 stalk celery, finely chopped
1 onion, finely chopped
Salt and pepper
Butter
Flour
Sweet or sour cream

Cook rice in consommé or beef broth until half-done. Remove the heavy part of the stems from the cabbage leaves, pour boiling water over the leaves and let stand while mixing the meat, parboiled rice, celery, onion, and seasonings. (If you're using leftover meat, you might want to add your favourite herbs as well.) Place 2 tablespoons of the mixture into each cabbage leaf (drained and dried); roll or fold the cabbage leaf round the meat mixture — securing with toothpicks if you like. Melt a generous piece of butter in an oven dish or roasting pan, place the cabbage rolls close together, but not on top of each other in the pan, and sprinkle with salt and pepper. Pour about 1 cupful of consommé or broth or tomato juice into pan, cover and bake at 300°F for about 45 minutes, adding more liquid; remove cover and continue baking and basting for another 30 minutes. Remove the rolls carefully, brown the juice in the pan (I add a bit of soy sauce), thicken with flour mixed with sweet or sour cream and pour over the cabbage rolls.

PAM NOONAN'S CABBAGE ROLLS

Pamela, who comes from Trinidad, said she was tired of being
served crumbly Octoberfest cabbage rolls that were mostly
rice; she devised this recipe of her own and brought a pot full
of rolls to my house on a January day when her writer-profes-
sor husband Gerry and her son Johnnie very kindly shovelled
deep snow off the roof of my cottage. Then we ate the best
cabbage rolls I've ever tasted.

Rolls:
3 pounds lean ground beef
2 small onions, chopped
2 eggs, well beaten
½ cup rice, cooked in bouillon
4 teaspoons soy sauce
¾ teaspoon tobasco sauce
½ teaspoon tarragon
¼ teaspoon cumin
Chopped chives
Salt, pepper, garlic salt, and celery salt

Cabbage leaves, parboiled

Sauce:
1 large can (28 oz.) tomato sauce
½ cup tomato ketchup
½ cup brown sugar
¼ cup vinegar
¼ cup prepared mustard
¼ cup barbeque sauce

Pam mixed well all the ingredients for the rolls then rolled two
rounded tablespoons of the mixture in each parboiled cabbage
leaf to make tight little bundles. She said you could secure them
with toothpicks but she didn't bother. While she was making
the rolls, she was simmering the ingredients for the sauce. She
put the rolls into her crockpot then poured the sauce over them.
She let it cook for about 10 hours; the rolls were firm and
delicious with plenty of sauce to cover each one. Pam said they
could be cooked in a heavy pot on a stove in less time — but
very slowly.

MAGGIE'S CABBAGE ROLL CASSEROLE

"Edna, who wants to fiddle around making all them cabbage rolls when they can make a casserole that tastes just as good?" Maggie asked me in her Neil's Harbour kitchen. Her son Keith echoed, "Mom, you said it."

1 pound ground beef
1 tablespoon oil
1 onion, finely sliced
⅛ teaspoon pepper
Salt
½ cup raw rice
1 can tomato soup
1 can water
3 cups shredded cabbage
Sour cream

In a large frying pan, brown the meat in oil for a few minutes. Add the onion, salt, pepper, and rice; mix well. While gently browning, add the soup and water. Put the cabbage in a baking dish, pour the rest over it and do not stir. Bake in a 325°F oven for 1½ hours. Put a dish of sour cream on the table to be spooned over each serving. "And that's some good," said Keith.

SALLY'S MEAT BALLS

Mother thought Sally Moogk was a wonderful cook.

¾ pound ground pork
¾ pound ground beef
2 eggs, beaten
1 onion, finely chopped
1 cup breadcrumbs
¾ cup rice, soaked in water
Salt and pepper
1 cup ketchup or tomato sauce

Mix all but the ketchup and form into balls; brown balls in a pan, put in an oven dish and cover with blended ketchup and one quart of boiling water. Let simmer in oven for 3 to 4 hours, making sure the balls haven't gone dry.

LUNENBURG SWEET AND SOUR MEATBALLS

A Lunenburg native told me this economical recipe is even better when reheated.

Meatballs:
1½ pounds ground beef
1 cup Rice Krispies
1 egg
1½ teaspoons salt
¼ teaspoon pepper
Pinch garlic salt

Sauce:
2 cups boiling water
¾ cup sugar
¼ cup vinegar
2 tablespoons soy sauce
2 tablespoons flour

Mix the ingredients for the meatballs. Divide into small balls. Fry them in a pan, using butter and oil, until they are brown on the outside. Boil the ingredients for the sauce for 10 minutes. Pour over the meatballs and let simmer for another 10 minutes. Serve with spaghetti, noodles, or rice.

SALLY'S ONE-DISH SUPPER OR LUNCHEON

We agreed with Mother that Sally was a good cook.

1¾ cups macaroni
½ pound sausages
1 green pepper, sliced
3 tablespoons butter
3 tablespoons flour
1½ cups milk
½ pound cheese
Salt and pepper

Boil the macaroni in a large amount of rapidly boiling, salted water, uncovered, until tender; drain, rinse with hot water and drain again. Leave 5 or 6 sausages whole and cut the remaining into ½-inch pieces; fry together until richly browned; remove from dripping.

Add green pepper to the sausage dripping and fry gently until pepper is tender. Arrange the cooked macaroni, half the green pepper, and the sausage pieces in layers in a greased casserole. Melt the butter; remove from heat and blend in the flour; gradually blend in the milk; cook, stirring constantly, until thickened.

Shred the cheese and reserve ½ a cup for topping. Add the remaining cheese to the cream sauce and stir until the cheese is melted; season to taste with salt and pepper. Pour sauce over the macaroni mixture in the casserole. Top the casserole with remaining green pepper and fried whole sausages. Bake uncovered in a 350°F oven for 20 minutes. Sprinkle with the ½ cup of cheese, return to the oven and bake until the cheese is melted — about 10 minutes longer.

SCALLOPED CORN BEEF

Lorna likes this easy-to-make supper dish with a green salad and mushroom muffins, hot and buttery.

>   1½ tablespoons butter
>   ½ small onion, finely chopped
>   ⅓ cup chopped celery
>   2 tablespoons flour
>   1½ cups milk
>   ½ teaspoon salt
>   ⅛ teaspoon pepper
>   1 medium can corned beef
>   Buttered crumbs

Melt the butter in a skillet, add the onion and celery; cook until the onion is soft and yellow. Add the flour and blend well, pour in the milk and cook to a smooth sauce. Season with salt and pepper, then stir in the corned beef broken into small pieces. Blend and place in a buttered baking dish. Sprinkle with buttered crumbs and bake in a 375°F oven for 25 minutes, while your muffins are baking as well.

SAUSAGE IN CORNBREAD

This is a perfect luncheon dish served with a salad or relishes and pickled things. Kit McDermott brought it to my house one Sunday when Françoise and Florence Dehlemmes from Brittany were visiting. Four of us ate every crumb.

> 1 piece of sausage, long enough to fit
>   exactly into a loaf pan
> 1 cup flour
> ½ teaspoon baking soda
> 1 tablespoon baking powder
> 2 tablespoons sugar
> 1 teaspoon dried basil or several fresh leaves
> 1 cup cornmeal
> 1 egg, beaten
> 1½ cups buttermilk
> ¼ cup grated Cheddar cheese
> ¼ cup melted butter

Peel the skin off the sausage if it is too tough to cut and to eat easily. Blend the flour, baking soda, baking powder, sugar, basil, and cornmeal. Combine the egg and buttermilk and stir into the dry ingredients. Stir in the Cheddar cheese and melted butter. Pour half the batter into a greased loaf pan. Place the sausage on top and cover it with the remaining batter. Bake at 400°F for 35 to 40 minutes or until the loaf has risen and is set. It will be soft and moist and crumbly when it is served.

Because Kit likes this so well, she makes it often and thinks she has improved it by cutting the sausage into bite-size pieces and stirring them into the cornmeal batter before she bakes it.

DISHES WITH PASTA OR NOODLES

In Waterloo there is a little Italian food shop where the proprietor will tell you that his favourite way to prepare and eat pasta is simply to boil it in salted water till tender, drain it, then mix it with melted butter and sprinkle it with lots of freshly ground parmesan cheese.

With a green salad, what more do you need for lunch?

BELLE'S BEEF AND PORK-SAUSAGE CASSEROLE

This is slightly sophisticated and very flavourful.

> ½ **pound spaghetti (or 1 package noodles)**
> ¾ **pound ground beef**
> ¾ **pound pork sausage meat**
> 1 **clove garlic, cut very fine**
> 1 **teaspoon salt**
> **Pepper**
> ½ **cup sliced mushrooms (or more)**
> ¼ **cup fresh lemon juice**
> 2 **cups spaghetti sauce**
> 4 **tablespoons crumbled blue cheese**
> 2 **tablespoons slivered almonds**

Cook noodles or spaghetti (we use noodles). Brown meat with garlic, salt, and pepper, then drain off fat. To meat, add mushrooms and lemon juice; blend in spaghetti sauce and simmer for 20 minutes. Add blue cheese. Mix with noodles — being careful not to overdo it. Bake at 375°F for 25 minutes. Sprinkle slivered almonds over the top and brown slightly.

MARJE MOYER'S CHICKEN CASSEROLE

This makes enough for a lot of people — a real Sunday company supper.

> 2 **chickens, boiled**
> 2 **cups chicken broth**
> 1 **can mushroom soup**
> 1 **can evaporated milk**
> 3 **tablespoons cornstarch**
> 2 **pounds mushrooms, sliced**
> 1 **green pepper, sliced**
> 2 **tablespoons butter**
> 6 **cups cooked noodles**
> 1 **cup breadcrumbs**

Cut the chickens into bite-sized pieces; combine the broth, soup, milk, and cornstarch in a saucepan on top of the stove. Heat and stir until thickened. Sauté the mushrooms and pepper in butter and add to sauce. Put chicken and noodles in a casserole. Pour sauce on top and cover with breadcrumbs. Put the casserole into a 350°F oven for about 45 minutes to heat through and brown the breadcrumbs. Serve with a salad, hot rolls, a vegetable, and sours. Apple halves sprinkled with sugar and cinnamon are nice with it too.

EASY NOODLE STROGANOFF

This dandy top-of-the-stove meal can be prepared in a jiffy. It can be easily cut in half — but it reheats very well. It has great flavour and is a godsend when someone comes unexpectedly for a meal.

   1 pound ground beef
   1 cup chopped or sliced onions
   4 cups canned or fresh tomatoes
   2 teaspoons Worcestershire sauce
   1 teaspoon salt
   Pepper
   ½ pound noodles
   1 cup sour cream

In a heavy pot over medium heat, sauté the beef and onions until browned, then pour off excess fat. Stir in tomatoes and Worcestershire sauce; sprinkle with salt and pepper. Bring to a boil. Add the noodles a few at a time so the mixture keeps on boiling. Reduce heat to low, cover, and simmer for 10 minutes longer, stirring occasionally, until the noodles are tender. Stir in the sour cream. Heat thoroughly, being careful not to boil the cream. Garnish with parsley.

BEEF CASSEROLE

Mardi Kersel, next door, thinks this is the best there is. Norm often makes it, too.

> **1½ to 2 pounds ground beef**
> **2 or 3 large onions, chopped**
> **¾ package large noodles, cooked**
> **1 or 2 cans mushrooms**
> **3 or 4 tablespoons chopped green pepper**
> **1 large can tomatoes**
> **1 pound grated cheese (plus some on top)**
> **Breadcrumbs**

Cook the meat in a frying pan until it's brown. Add the onions and cook until transparent. Combine everything but the breadcrumbs; mix but don't stir too much or you will break up the noodles and the dish will be mushy. Put the mixture into a big casserole, cover with a topping of cheese and breadcrumbs and bake in a 350°F oven for about 45 minutes. You can add a few other things to this if you like — I always put in some soy sauce.

BEEF MACARONI CASSEROLE

An easy and filling family supper dish.

> **½ pound macaroni**
> **1 pound ground beef**
> **1 cup chopped onion**
> **Salt and pepper**
> **1 can cream of mushroom soup**
> **1 cup sour cream**
> **1 tablespoon sherry**
> **2 cups green peas**

In a large pot of salted water, boil the macaroni till tender. Drain. In a skillet, brown the beef and onions over medium heat. Sprinkle with salt and papper. Stir in the soup and simmer for 10 minutes. Remove from heat and stir in the sour cream, sherry, macaroni, and peas. Pour into a casserole and bake at 350°F for about 35 minutes, or until brown on top.

BAKED NOODLES WITH CHEESE AND SHERRY

Of course, you could omit the sherry and use milk instead but you would lose that subtle flavour.

½ package wide egg noodles
2 tablespoons butter
2 tablespoons flour
1 cup sour cream
1 cup dry sherry
1 cup cottage or Cheddar cheese
1 teaspoon Worcestershire sauce
1 teaspoon paprika
Pinch garlic powder
Salt and pepper
Sprinkle grated Parmesan or Cheddar cheese

Cook the noodles in a large pot of boiling water until tender; drain. Melt butter; stir in flour. Add sour cream and sherry, stirring over low heat until thickened — but don't boil. Remove from heat, add cottage cheese, Worcestershire sauce, paprika, garlic powder, salt, and pepper. Stir in the noodles. Turn into a buttered baking dish. Sprinkle with cheese and bake at 350°F, uncovered, for about 40 minutes, or until noodles are hot and top is golden brown.

Kit and Vern and I ate every bit of this at a sitting — with crisp coleslaw.

FRANKFURTER CHEESE BAKE

You can double this if you want to serve six. With a green salad it's an easy meal for three, or for two with one left over for tomorrow.

¼ pound egg noodles
¾ cup grated cheese
1 tablespoon flour
Pinch salt
½ cup milk
2 tablespoons melted butter
½ pound of frankfurters, sliced
2 tablespoons brown sugar
2 tablespoons mayonnaise
1 teaspoon mustard

Cook the noodles in a large pot of boiling salted water, then drain. Combine cheese, flour, salt, and milk in a bowl. Carefully stir it and the melted butter into noodles. Pour into a buttered shallow baking pan.

Mix remaining ingredients, and spoon evenly over noodles. Bake at 375°F for 20 minutes, or until hot and bubbly.

FRIED NOODLES

Sometimes Mother served these instead of potatoes with chops, chicken, or steaks, but mostly we had them with cold meats and a salad for supper.

Sometimes butter is merely allowed to melt over the hot, boiled noodles, and they are covered, before serving, with browned buttered crumbs, or sprinkled with parsley.

To fry noodles: melt two tablespoons of **butter** in a pan and pour the **cooked noodles** into it; to keep them separate and slippery, stir them around in the pan until they are golden.

Or pour the noodles into the butter in the pan and put on a lid, letting the noodles become brown on the bottom, very, very slowly; then flip the whole mass over and let the other side become golden too. You may need to add more butter. The noodles will become one piece, which can be cut to serve.

DEUTSCHER NOODLE RING

You can have this for "fancy," trimming it up as much as you like.

>   **1 cup noodles**
>   **2 tablespoons butter**
>   **3 tablespoons flour**
>   **1½ cups milk**
>   **¼ or ½ pound cheese, cubed**
>   **Salt and pepper**
>   **2 eggs, well beaten**

Boil the noodles in salted water and cook till tender. Drain and put into a well-greased ring mould. Melt the butter, add the flour, and blend. Stir in the milk and stir constantly until the sauce thickens. Add the cheese, salt, and pepper. Reserve half the sauce to use later. To the remaining sauce, add the well-beaten eggs and mix well. Pour the sauce over the noodles, set the mould in a pan of hot water, and bake in a 350°F oven for about 45 minutes. Unmould on a large platter, fill the centre with vegetables, meat, or seafood, then pour the remaining hot cheese sauce over the noodle ring.

NOODLES ROMANOFF

I don't know what the Romanoffs had to do with this, but I know your guests — or family — will have more than one helping if you serve it with cold meat and a salad.

>   **1 package noodles**
>   **4 cups sour cream**
>   **1½ cups shredded sharp Cheddar cheese**
>   **1 bunch green onions, sliced across stems**
>   **Salt and pepper**
>   **Paprika**

Cook the noodles in salted water till soft. Drain. Blend the sour cream, 1 cup of the cheese, onion, salt, and pepper. Stir gently into the noodles without mushing them. Put all into a casserole, top with remaining cheese and sprinkle with paprika. Cover, refrigerate several hours, or overnight. Bake, uncovered, in a 350°F oven for 40 minutes till heated through.

SPAGHETTI AND MEATBALLS

I'm giving you this because so many people have told me they couldn't find a recipe for this filling dish. Stan Hutton says it is his specialty and he's proud of it.

Sauce:
4 cups tomatoes, canned or fresh or frozen
1 cup water
¾ cup chopped onion
1 clove garlic, minced
3 tablespoons olive oil
1 tablespoon sugar
1½ teaspoons crushed oregano
1½ teaspoons salt
½ teaspoon pepper
1 bay leaf

Meatballs:
4 slices dry bread
1 pound ground beef
2 eggs
½ cup grated cheese
2 tablespoons chopped parsley
1 clove garlic, minced
1 teaspoon crushed oregano
1 teaspoon salt
Dash pepper

2 tablespoons vegetable oil
1 pound spaghetti

Blend all sauce ingredients together. Bring to a boil, and then let simmer while you make the meatballs.

Soak the bread in water for 2 or 3 minutes, then squeeze out the moisture. Combine the soaked bread with remaining ingredients except oil and spaghetti; mix well. Form into about 20 small balls. Brown slowly in hot cooking oil then put the meat balls in the sauce and simmer for about 30 minutes.

Meanwhile, boil the spaghetti until tender, about 12 minutes. Serve the meatballs and sauce over the spaghetti and eat plenty with a free conscience.

BETSY BRUBACHER'S SPAGHETTI

Wonderful to make when you have to feed a lot of people — it's easy, expandable, and everyone loves it with a green salad and a red wine.

1 pound spaghetti
4 medium-sized onions, sliced
2 small green peppers, cut up
¼ cup vegetable oil
4 cups canned or fresh tomatoes
2 teaspoons salt
½ cup grated or cubed cheese
5 or 6 bay leaves
Bacon slices

Cook the long strings of spaghetti in boiling, salted water until tender. Drain. Cook the sliced onions and peppers in the vegetable oil, gently, until partly cooked; add the tomatoes and salt and cook till the onions are tender. Add the cheese to the drained spaghetti and put it into an ovenware serving dish. Pour the tomato mixture over it, inserting the bay leaves where you can pick them out before you serve the spaghetti. Spread bacon slices over the top of the spaghetti and put the covered dish into a 250 to 300°F oven; leaving it as long as you need to. If it dries out a bit you can always add more tomato juice. Before serving, take off the lid to crisp the bacon (you may need to grill extra bacon).

GREEN RICE

Parsley is supposed to be very good for you. This should give you plenty, and remember that millions of people live mostly on rice.

> 1 cup long-grain rice
> 4 cups boiling water
> 1 teaspoon salt
> 3 eggs
> 2 cups cream
> ½ cup melted butter
> 1 cup grated sharp Cheddar cheese
> 2 cups finely minced parsley
> 1 medium onion, grated
> 2 cloves garlic, minced
> Salt and pepper

Cook the rice in boiling salted water until tender but firm, about 20 minutes. Drain. Keep hot. In a small bowl, beat the eggs until light, then add cream, butter, cheese, parsley, onion, garlic, and seasonings. Mix well. Stir mixture into the rice, then put into a buttered casserole. Bake at 350°F for about one hour or until firm.

QUICHES, SAVOURY PIES, AND PIZZA

Somebody once wrote a book called Real Men Don't Eat Quiche. *But don't you believe it. Whenever I've baked and served a quiche, the men have wanted second and third helpings.*

There's nothing like a quiche for a company luncheon, a family meal, or a buffet supper. Quiches are easy to make, to serve, to eat — and everyone loves them.

With a pat-in pastry crust they can be made in a jiffy. The crust can even be prepared in advance — the day before the event — a filling can be assembled a few hours ahead and put together quickly just before guests arrive. The quiche can be baking with a tantalizing aroma while you serve a glass of sherry. It can be kept hot, or can be frozen and rewarmed without loss of flavour or favour.

Quiches can be so verstile. Though their base is always eggs and milk, their main ingredients can be whatever you choose: ham, bacon, cheese, onions, corn, asparagus, broccoli, green peppers, mushrooms, chicken, tuna, shrimp, salmon, lobster, crab-meat, hamburger, or whatever, and innumerable combinations.

Use the following ham quiche recipe and merely substitute any other ingredient to have a different quiche. After you get the hang of it, there'll be no stopping you.

PAT-IN PASTRY

This needs no rolling, has no little bits of pastry left over, and can be prepared in a 9-inch quiche pan or deep pie plate almost as quickly as it takes to tell you how to do it.

> 1½ cups sifted flour — all-purpose or
>   whole-wheat or a combination
> 1½ teaspoons sugar
> ½ teaspoon salt
> ½ cup oil
> 3 tablespoons cold milk — sometimes a bit more

Sift the flour, sugar, and salt directly into the quiche pan or pie plate. Combine the oil and milk in a measuring cup and beat with a fork until creamy. Pour all at once over the flour. Mix with a fork until the flour is completely dampened. Push the dough with your fingers to line the bottom and sides of the plate.

Or put all the ingredients into your food processer, give it a quick whirl, then scrape it into the quiche pan and pat it in. Flute the edges. Pour in the quiche filling and bake it.

The crust will be crisp, tender, and tasty.

CAROL'S SALMON QUICHE

A salmon couldn't have a better finale than this. It is super.

> 1 cup chopped or shredded Cheddar cheese
> Pastry for a 9- or 10-inch pie plate
> 2 tablespoons chopped onion
> 2 small cans salmon drained,
>   reserve liquid
> 3 eggs
> 1 cup milk
> ¼ teaspoon basil, tarragon, or oregano

Strew the cheese over the bottom of the pastry shell, sprinkle it with the onion, and arrange the flaked salmon over the onion to cover right to the edge. In a bowl, mix eggs, the salmon liquid, and milk. Pour evenly over the salmon. Sprinkle with the basil, tarragon, or oregano. Bake at 375°F for about 55 minutes, or until set. Serve hot in wedges with a green vegetable, or salad — or both.

QUICHE LORRAINE

Sounds too sophisticated to be a Mennonite dish but it did originate in the Vosges Mountains where many of the Mennonites lived in the days of their religious persecution.

Pastry for a deep pie plate
1 cup shredded Swiss cheese
   (I've often done it with mild Cheddar)
6 slices bacon
6 eggs
½ teaspoon salt
A slight sprinkle of nutmeg
1 tablespoon Kirsch
½ cup milk
½ cup cream

Line a deep pie pan with pastry. Sprinkle a ½ cup of shredded cheese evenly on the bottom. Cut bacon into bits and fry until it has lost about half its fat. Distribute the bacon bits on top of the cheese and sprinkle 2 tablespoons of the bacon fat on top. Into a bowl break the eggs; beat them, add salt, pepper, and nutmeg, then the Kirsch, milk, cream, and the rest of the bacon and shredded cheese. Blend; then carefully pour this mixture over the bacon and cheese in the pie. Bake it on the floor of your oven at 350°F for 40 to 50 minutes.

Your guests won't want more than one glass of sherry when they catch a whiff of the quiche in the oven. Serve immediately when you take it out, puffed-up and golden; it will flatten if you keep it waiting — but it will still taste good.

VARIATION

One day when I was having guests for lunch I decided I'd better have two quiches, one for seconds. I had 2 cobs of fresh corn left from dinner the night before; I cut off the kernels, fried them for a few minutes in bacon fat, then spread them (instead of bacon) over the cheese in the pie shell before I poured in the egg and milk mixture. The ladies were just as enthusiastic about their seconds as they had been about their firsts.

HAM QUICHE

Got some ham left over from a big company or family dinner? This is a great way to revitalize it. Freeze the ham, and when you plan to make a quiche let the ham thaw a bit. Slice off enough round the edges to make a cupful when chopped and quickly put the rest of the chunk back into the freezer before it has a chance to thaw. You can make quite a few delicious quiches this way. Or keep a tin of flaked ham in your emergency cupboard and use it for a quiche. This quiche is easy if you use your food processor to grate the cheese and cut up the onion and ham.

> **Pastry for 9-inch pie plate or quiche dish**
> **(use Pat-In Pastry on page 28)**
> **½ cup finely sliced onions (more or less)**
> **1 cup grated Cheddar cheese (more or less)**
> **1 cup diced ham (more or less)**
> **2 eggs, beaten**
> **2 tablespoons flour**
> **1 cup milk**
> **Pepper**

In the pastry shell, spread the onion. Sprinkle with grated cheese, then the ham. In a bowl, blend the eggs, flour, and milk; sprinkle with pepper. (The cheese and ham are probably salty enough to skip the salt.) When you are ready to bake the quiche, pour the egg mixture carefully into the pastry shell almost to the brim. Put a pan under it in the oven for overflow. Bake at 400°F for 10 minutes. Then at 350°F for about 30 minutes more — but have a look before that. When it seems solid — or when a knife inserted comes out clean and the pastry looks done — take it from the oven and serve it piping hot with a tossed, bean, or cabbage salad. Be prepared to serve second helpings. You may need more than one quiche.

POTATO CRUST QUICHE

This is a very good quiche and not much more bother to make than one with a pastry crust.

Crust:
3 cups finely shredded raw potato
3 tablespoons vegetable oil

Filling:
1 large onion, grated
1 cup grated cheese
1 cup slivered ham (or chicken or sausage or
  salmon or tuna)
2 eggs
½ cup milk

To make the crust, mix the shredded potatoes and oil in a bowl, then press into a buttered quiche dish or a 9-inch pie plate. Bake at 425°F for 15 minutes.

Spread the onion over the bottom of the half-baked potato crust. Cover with cheese, then spread the ham on top of the cheese. Beat the eggs until light and blend in the milk. Pour slowly over the ham. Add more milk if necessary to almost fill the dish. Bake at 350°F for about 30 minutes, or until quiche is golden brown. This quiche reheats quite nicely, if necessary.

DUTCH BEEF PIE

Bevvy makes this with leftover meat or raw ground beef.

1 pound ground beef
1 cup chopped celery
1 cup chopped onion
½ teaspoon mustard
Salt and pepper
2 tablespoons flour
1 cup water
Pastry for double crust pie

Mix the meat, vegetables, and seasonings and brown lightly in a frying pan. Lower heat and cook for about 10 minutes more. Sprinkle mixture with flour, mix well and add water, stir and cook a few minutes longer. Cool thoroughly and the mixture will be fairly thick. Then pour it into the pastry-lined pie plate, cover it with the top crust, make slits for steam, and bake at 425°F for about 30 minutes. With it you need only a salad for a good supper.

JEAN SALTER'S SUSSEX PIE

A nice luncheon dish for two with a green salad

> **1 onion, chopped**
> **2 tablespoons butter**
> **½ cup grated cheese**
> **1 cup breadcrumbs**
> **Salt and pepper**
> **2 tomatoes, sliced**
> **2 eggs, beaten**
> **A little mustard**

Fry the onion in butter. Mix the grated cheese and breadcrumbs, season with salt and pepper. Put alternate layers of sliced tomatoes, fried onions, cheese, and breadcrumb mixture in a pie dish, ending with breadcrumbs. Pour the beaten eggs and mustard over all. Bake in a 425°F oven for 15 to 20 minutes. Watch that it doesn't burn.

JEAN SALTER'S CHEESE AND EGG PIE

You might call it a quiche — but why? This is English.

> **1½ cups grated cheese**
> **2 tablespoons flour**
> **9-inch pie shell**
> **2 tablespoons butter**
> **4 eggs**
> **2 cups milk**
> **1 teaspoon salt**
> **¼ teaspoon pepper**

Mix the cheese and flour and spread in the pie shell. Add butter in bits. In a mixing bowl, beat the eggs, add the milk, salt, and pepper, and stir until smooth. Pour over the cheese mixture in the pie shell. Bake in a 350°F oven for about 40 minutes or until it is puffed and brown. Remove, cool for 10 minutes before cutting into wedges for six.

ONION PIE

A sort of quiche that would be great to serve to guests at lunch or as a supper dish for the family.

1 cup crushed crackers
4 tablespoons melted butter

Combine and press in bottom and sides of a 9-inch pie plate, or use a pastry crust.

6 slices bacon, cut up
1 cup chopped onion
2 cups shredded cheese
¼ cup sour cream
2 eggs, slightly beaten
Dash pepper
Chopped pimiento (optional)
Cheese slices

In a skillet, cook bacon till crisp; remove bacon and pour off all the fat but 2 tablespoons. In the bacon fat, cook onion until tender, not brown. Combine onion, bacon, and shredded cheese, add sour cream, eggs, pepper, and, if you want a touch of colour, the chopped pimiento. Put all in the pie shell, bake at 375°F for 35 to 45 minutes. Take it from the oven and put slices of cheese — or more shredded cheese — on top, then back in the oven for 2 or 3 minutes. Remove and let it stand for 10 minutes before serving. This recipe could easily be doubled for 2 pies.

PIZZA

Next time you make bread, whack off enough of the risen dough to make a pizza or two. You'll need just enough to flatten into a pizza pan, a pie plate, or a cookie sheet. You'll probably stop ordering take-out pizza after you've tried your own invention.

If you like, you can make dough especially for pizza:

> **1 tablespoon yeast**
> **1 cup lukewarm water or milk**
> **1 teaspoon sugar**
> **1 teaspoon salt**
> **2 tablespoons oil or melted shortening**
> **2 cups flour**

Dissolve the yeast in the warm milk with the sugar (unless you have instant yeast, which can be added with the flour). Add the salt, shortening, and flour, mix well, and knead a few times till the dough is elastic. Roll out about ½-inch thick and flatten on a pizza pan or pie plate or on a cookie sheet, forming a rim round the edge. Let rise in a warm place for about an hour.

Meantime, you can assemble whatever you like to have on a pizza. Think of what you order when you go to a pizza palace and try to duplicate it.

Or invent your own pizza, remembering that almost anything goes. Spread the dough with **tomato sauce or tomato paste, or even ketchup.** Sprinkle it with whatever you choose: **mushrooms, ground meat, or sliced wieners or pepperoni or summer sausage, or anchovies or shrimp, green peppers, sliced olives, oregano, basil.** Anything else you can think of? Now cover generously with sliced or grated **Mozzarella cheese.** Thin slices of **tomato** sprinkled with **Parmesan** cheese add a nice touch.

Bake at 425°F for 20 to 25 minutes — until the crust is golden and the filling is bubbly. Have fun and good luck.

MEAT LOAVES

HAM LOAF

Mother was very proud of this when she had people for Sunday-night supper.

1 cup pineapple rings, drained
Maraschino cherries
¼ cup brown sugar
3 pounds ham, chopped
2 slices bread, cut in cubes
2 eggs
¾ cup milk
1 tablespoon butter
1 teaspoon pepper
1 teaspoon vinegar
1 teaspoon prepared mustard

Line a loaf pan with waxed paper, place pineapple rings and cherries in a pattern around sides and bottom; sprinkle them with brown sugar. Mix up all the rest and press into the loaf pan — being careful not to disturb the fruit. Bake at 350°F for 1 hour.

FRESH HAM LOAF

For flavour, this ham loaf was even better.

1½ pounds ground pork
1½ pounds ground cured pork
3 cups breadcrumbs
1 cup tomato juice
3 eggs — large ones
Salt and pepper

Mix all together and bake 1½ hours at 350° to 400°F.

"CHELLIED" CHICKEN

Of this cold chicken loaf, Bevvy says, "I generally make it with the parts of the chicken that aren't so nice to put on the table to eat so, but it's even nicer yet if you use the whole chicken."

1 small chicken or pieces
¼ teaspoon pepper
2 tablespoons gelatine

Cook the chicken in salted water until it is tender enough to fall off the bones. Take it out of the broth and reserve broth. Remove the bones. Cut the meat into pieces and put it in a loaf pan or a mould or individual dishes. You might want to put a few green peas, pimiento bits, pepper rings, or slices of hard-boiled egg in the bottom "for nice," Bevvy says.

Remove the fat from the broth. Dissolve the gelatine in ½ cup of cold water, then in 5 cups, more or less, of the hot chicken broth. Pour the mixture over the meat, mix well together, and pour or spoon it into the moulds. Put it in a cool place till you want to use it. Unmould on a serving plate and garnish as fancily as you please.

JELLIED VEAL LOAF

This decorative, mildly flavoured loaf usually accompanied a ham as a contrast in colour and taste when Mother had a buffet supper.

**3 pounds veal (or 1 pound lean veal and
    1 veal knuckle)
1 large onion finely chopped
2 stalks celery, chopped
1 tablespoon butter
Salt and pepper
1 tablespoon gelatine (not needed if you use the
    veal knuckle)
2 hard-boiled eggs
1 tablespoon cut-up parsley**

Cut the veal into pieces, add the onion, celery, butter, and seasoning. Cover with water and let it cook slowly — about 2½ hours — or until the meat is tender and the liquid reduced to about 2 cups. If you don't have the veal knuckle, soak the gelatine in ½ cup cold water for 5 minutes. Grind, chop, or shred the veal. Strain the hot stock and dissolve the gelatine in it. Add the chopped veal and mix well. Place hard-boiled egg slices and chopped parsley in the bottom of a mould or loaf pan and pour the veal mixture carefully over it. Put it in a cool place for several hours to jell. Unmould it onto a serving dish and slice it with a sharp knife. If you'd rather, you could make individual moulds and decorate them prettily on a plate.

Entertaining

*I object to the word "entertaining" when it is applied to
inviting friends to my house for tea or a meal. I don't
entertain them, put on a display, show off my possessions,
impress them with culinary skills. I invite them because I
like them and want to spend some time with them talking,
listening, and laughing. I invite them because I want to be
with them, not in my kitchen fussing over dishes that need
much of my time.*

*When I was first married, I used to be nervous when I'd
invited people to come to our house; I was afraid
everything wouldn't be perfect. I spent hours preparing
and then running from the living or dining room to my
kitchen. But the Second World War brought so many
droppers-in to our house that I had no chance to prepare
ahead. I just served what I had or could prepare at a
moment's notice. I learned to be casual, to enjoy my
visitors. I hoped they came to be with me, not to be given a
feast. I always had bread and butter and a tin of sardines,
and if I didn't I could quickly stir up some biscuits or
muffins. I always had spaghetti or noodles and apples,
summer sausage, and pickles. Now I have a freezer that I
can call on in an emergency.*

*When I lived in the city our house — which I'd planned
— had the kitchen so far from the living room that I
couldn't hear conversations going on there. I was always
frustrated.*

*When I planned the cottage where I live now, I made sure
I could be with my visitors at all times. The kitchen is at
the end of my living room. A door and three large windows
along the counter open into the summer room. I am never
out of the sight or hearing of my friends. Time spent in my
kitchen is not wasted or resented, but I still like to
minimize it by preparing food that is simple and easy to
serve without much distraction.*

FOR VEGETARIANS — OR ANYONE ELSE

VEGETABLE LOAF

This combination of vegetables and nuts is interesting and sufficiently satisfying to make you not miss the meat in what looks like a meat loaf.

> 4 medium-sized carrots
> 3 large boiled potatoes
> 2 medium onions
> 1 cup salted peanuts
> 1 cup celery
> 1 cup spinach or cabbage
> 2 tablespoons parsley
> 1 cup whole-wheat breadcrumbs
> ½ cup milk
> 3 eggs, slightly beaten
> 1 teaspoon salt
> Pepper

In a chopping bowl or food processor, chop up very fine the carrots, potatoes, onions, peanuts, celery, spinach or cabbage, and parsley. While you are chopping, soak the breadcrumbs in the milk. Stir all together, add the slightly beaten eggs, salt, and pepper, and mix thoroughly. Butter a loaf pan and pat the mixture into it. (You might dot a bit of butter on top if you like.) Bake at 350°F for about an hour and a half. The top should be brown and the loaf firm. It is good hot or cold and might be served with mushroom or tomato sauce (pages 88 and 89) and a tossed salad. All very nutritious and delicious.

MEATLESS MEAT LOAF

I doubled this for three members of an ashram in Toronto who stayed at my house after telling the K-W University Women's Club about their belief in yoga. They all rose at dawn to meditate and one young man offered to anoint my feet with oil.

    1 cup chopped mixed nuts
    1 cup whole-wheat breadcrumbs
    1 cup cooked rice
    1 onion, chopped
    3 tablespoons melted butter
    ½ teaspoon crumbled dry basil
    ¼ teaspoon crumbled thyme
    Squirt of Worcestershire sauce
    Salt and pepper

Mix all the ingredients, add a little water to moisten. Press into a buttered loaf pan, bake in a 375°F oven for 35 minutes, dotting with additional melted butter. Serve with or without mushroom or tomato sauce (pages 88 and 89), and a green salad.

VEGETABLE WALNUT LOAF

Nancy and her vegetarian friends really liked this when I tried it on them. It's light and has lots of flavour — almost meaty, I'd say.

    1½ cups soft breadcrumbs, whole wheat preferred
    1 cup walnuts
    1 medium onion, cut in chunks
    1½ cups cooked sliced carrots
    3 eggs, slightly beaten
    1½ cups milk
    1½ cups cooked or canned peas
    2 tablespoons melted butter
    1½ teaspoons salt
    Pepper

You may put all this into your blender or food processor until it is finely chopped — or you may do the job with a grinder or a sharp knife. Mix all together thoroughly, pack it into a well-buttered loaf pan, 9" x 5", and bake at 350°F for an hour. Serve with a sauce if you like and a good leafy salad.

NANCY'S CARROT LOAF

Nancy writes about this: "At the last minute, discovering I have few ingredients, I can always make this carrot loaf and ensure compliments from my guests. Served with hot muffins, it's a simple and delicious meal. It's also a great way to get rid of old tired carrots."

3 eggs, beaten
1½ cups stewed tomatoes
1 tablespoon honey
1 onion, grated
2 or more cups grated carrot
½ cup raisins
⅓ cup soy flour (or whole wheat)
1 cup breadcrumbs (whole wheat)
½ teaspoon salt
3 tablespoons Brewers' yeast
   (optional for health freaks)
¼ cup sunflower seeds
½ teaspoon marjoram

Beat the eggs, add tomatoes, honey, onion, carrots, and raisins. In another bowl mix flour, breadcrumbs, salt, yeast, sunflower seeds, and marjoram. Combine the wet ingredients with the dry ones and stir well. Bake at 350°F for 1 hour or more until the eggs set. "If you have good luck turning the loaf upside down, you will be very pleased with the visual effect," Nancy says.

Switzerland Lunch

Often when I am alone and knitting, I like to muse over memorable meals I have had in various places in the world. One I recall most fondly was a lunch in Switzerland with my friend Alphonse Ludaescher.

We had gone up a mountainside by funicular and had walked perhaps a mile along a green path till we came to a mountain meadow that was covered with purple, yellow, and white crocuses. We couldn't sit without crushing them. But we did sit and look across the Lauterbrunnen Valley at the Pride of the Swiss Oberland — the Jungfrau, the Munsch, and the Eiger, their glaciers gleaming in the spring sunshine, one of the world's most glorious sights.

At noon Alphonse opened his backpack and brought out a bottle of Chianti, fresh golden brodchen, several kinds of Swiss cheese, a tube of strawberry jam, and bars of Toblerone chocolate. A feast for the gods. And during those moments we were on the top of the world.

CRÊPES GRUYÈRE

The mother of my friend in Switzerland one day took us to a restaurant in Montreux where the specialty was Crêpes Gruyère: pieces of cheese dipped in batter, deep fried crisp and golden, the cheese creamy soft inside. Maman was very fussy about what we ate with them: tender butter lettuce salad, white wine at room temperature, prunes stewed with an orange liqueur, and coffee. Of course, the restaurateur would not give his recipe; I've been trying ever since that memorable day to find something like it. I think this comes close. I wish I could also reproduce Montreux' promenade view of the snowcapped Dents du Midi across the turquoise-blue waters of lovely Lac Leman.

> 1 egg, beaten
> 1 tablespoon oil
> ½ teaspoon salt
> ¾ cup stale beer or white wine or milk
> 1 cup flour

**Pieces of Gruyère or any similar mild white cheese
cut in pieces 1" x 3" x ¾"**

Blend the first four ingredients then stir in the flour, using more or less till the batter is smooth and drops off the spoon with a splat, not a stream. Let the batter rest for a couple of hours, or overnight. Just before serving time, dip the pieces of cheese in the batter to coat them well, fry in hot fat until crisp and golden. As you eat them, I doubt if you'll miss those mountains at Montreux.

If you don't want to use up all the batter with the cheese, you might drop prunes or half-inch slices of apple or pieces of banana into it to make fritters.

Watch your deep fat frying. Don't do it unless you're going to stand right beside it every second. If your phone rings, turn off the heat before you answer. Let the crêpes die a natural death; better sacrifice them than take a chance on burning your house. Ever notice how many fires are started by french fries?

And never, never, never put a lid on the hot fat pot: it can explode when you remove it. I have a friend who was horribly burned when he did it — and so was his kitchen.

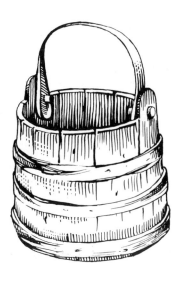

SWISS FONDUE

My friend in Lausanne, Switzerland, introduced me to Swiss Fondue. We would sit in a candle-lit restaurant with the bubbling cheese on the table between us and dip into it pieces of crusty French bread. According to Swiss tradition, whoever dropped a piece of bread from a fork into the fondue had to pay for the meal or give the other person a kiss. I seemed to always be the loser — one way or another.

1 clove garlic
1 cup dry white wine (preferably Neuchatel)
4 cups shredded Swiss cheese (preferably Gruyère)
1½ teaspoons cornstarch
2 tablespoons Kirsch
Pepper

Rub the inside of a saucepan or earthenware fondue dish or chafing dish with cut clove of garlic. Pour in the wine and heat but don't let it boil. Stir in about ¼ cup of cheese, stir vigorously. Keep adding in small amounts, stirring all the time until all the cheese is melted and the mixture is thoroughly blended. Add the cornstarch blended with the Kirsch and stir until the mixture bubbles. Sprinkle with a bit of pepper. Keep the fondue hot but not simmering over an alcohol burner with a low flame, or a low candle. If it becomes too thick, add a little more warm wine. Have French bread alongside torn into bite-sized pieces; put a piece on a fork, dip it in the fondue and don't burn your tongue when you eat it. You'll be amazed at how much you will consume. Don't underestimate.

NANCY'S FAVOURITE LASAGNA

Nancy writes: "Even hardy meat-eaters love this rich, cheesy dish. When I'm in the mood for a treat, I always think about cooking this recipe." There are 4 basic steps:

1. Make tomato sauce.
2. Cook lasagna noodles (1 box) and drain.
3. Grate and slice cheeses.
4. Assemble.

TOMATO SAUCE

I never worry about making too much of this sauce because it freezes well. Some day when I want to eat a good meal but am too lazy to prepare one, I go to the freezer and thaw this sauce. Then I put it on top of spaghetti with mushrooms, or cook brown rice and mix the two together. This sauce is easily improvised. The secret is in the spices.

In a large pan, boil slowly for about an hour:

> **3 cups stewed tomatoes (or fresh ones)**
> **1 small tin tomato paste**
> **1 cup cut-up carrots**
> **1 cup chopped onion**
> **1 cup chopped celery**
> **2 to 3 cloves garlic, minced**
> **1 large green pepper, chopped**
> **2 cups mushrooms, sliced**
> **2 tablespoons basil**
> **1 tablespoon oregano**
> **1 tablespoon marjoram**
> **1 teaspoon thyme**
> **1 teaspoon garlic powder**
> **Salt and pepper**

When sauce is cooked and cooled, mix it with **1 pound ricotta cheese**. If unavailable, use any kind of cream cheese or cottage cheese. Set aside until you are ready to layer.

Slice thinly **1 pound Mozzarella cheese**, grate finely ½ **pound Parmesan** or use packaged.

Begin to layer in a large and deep cake or loaf pan. I can often stretch this recipe into two pans and freeze one, depending on the number of people I am feeding. On the bottom of a greased pan, place a layer of **cooked noodles**, then smooth on a layer of sauce mixed with ricotta cheese. Then a layer of Mozzarella cheese, and last sprinkle with Parmesan. Continue these layers until the pan is nearly full. Bake at 350°F for 20 to 30 minutes. Needs only to be heated through and the cheeses melted.

SUPPER WITH LAWRENCE

I am so lucky. Occasionally my much-younger-than-I friends
call and ask if I'd like them to come to my house and make me a
supper. The first one to do it was Ashley Lubin, who made a
Chinese meal. He brought all the ingredients, candles, roses,
and a beautiful girl with a cloak of honey blonde hair and eyes
the colour of forget-me-nots.

Next came Lawrence McNaught: slim, with masses of curly
black hair, soft brown eyes, and a dreamy soft voice that re-
flects the accents of his Scottish father and Maltese mother.
With him came Paul, tall and handsome. They had a swim first
then drank wine and chatted till I wondered if the great bags of
groceries they'd brought were forgotten.

It was eight o'clock when they started. Paul peeled and sliced
4 or 5 onions. Lawrence sautéed them in **oil** with **garlic**, then
added a **large can of tomatoes** and a **small one of tomato
paste**. He tended it lovingly as it simmered while Paul cleaned
and took **mushrooms** off their stems (and would have thrown
them away but Lawrence rescued them for his sauce).

Under Lawrence's direction I chopped up **cauliflower tops**;
Paul cleaned **green peppers**, putting the seeds into Lawrence's
brew — they said the germ, the essence of anything, is in its
seeds which should never be discarded.

Next Lawrence put ¼ **cup cut parsley** and almost a **teaspoon
of basil** into his sauce with ½ **teaspoon coriander** and ½ tea-
spoon curry powder. "It smells kind of nice," he said. "Reminds
me of the sauce we made in Mexico by the side of a river with
turquoise water."

Paul tasted as he crumbled some **feta cheese**, putting cauliflower bits on thin slices and handing some to me, until Lawrence reminded him that he needed everything for his dish.

Lawrence put the cauliflower into the pepper cups with the
crumbled cheese, pieces of **canned pimiento** on top; he put the
pepper lids back on, perfectly matched, then dropped them
carefully into the tomato sauce. They floated — to his dismay.
He patted them down, put them in the oven at 350°F for about
an hour. Meantime Paul cooked **noodles**, putting a teaspoon of
oil in the water so the noodles wouldn't stick.

At 11:15 our dinner was ready. Green peppers with the sauce spooned over the noodles, sprinkled with Parmesan. With wine. And very good, too. For dessert Lawrence brought expensive Byng cherries dipped in pure thick sweet cream. We finished dining at midnight. Nancy was amazed! She told me, "When Lawrence has a dinner party at his house he starts preparing the food after everyone gets there. That is the evening's entertainment. We sometimes don't eat until two in the morning."

EGG DISHES

Eating In Paris

The first time I went to Europe I sailed on the old Queen Elizabeth, landed at Cherbourg, and took the boat train to Paris, where I stayed on a street so narrow that I couldn't take a picture of La Princesse, my small hotel near the notorious cafés Flore and Les Deux Magots on St. Germaine de Près. Excited, thrilled, and sometimes a bit nervous, for eight days I strolled round the old streets near the Seine. I couldn't spend much money because I was just beginning three months of wandering by myself on the continent and I didn't know how long my money would last.

My school French wasn't that great but I managed fairly well, except in restaurants where I couldn't translate the menus. Every morning I went to a different little café and ordered hot chocolate and a croissant, flaky and warm from the oven. At noon I'd go into a shop and buy cheese and petit pains or a savoury tart to eat on a bench or a stone wall while I watched the barges on the river or the people of Paris passing by. Then I'd find a patisserie where I splurged on florentines or pastries.

By evening I was hungry and would go to a restaurant for a proper meal. But because I couldn't translate the menu and dinners were expensive, I ordered an omelette and lettuce salad — every night. I have never tasted such delicious omelettes; each one seemed the best I'd ever eaten. I always wondered how the chefs achieved such perfection — with fine herbes, fromage (I knew that meant cheese), jambon (that was ham). They were served like magic, almost instantly, with a tender leaf lettuce salad glistening in its dressing of oil and vinegar.

But think of the wasted opportunity to eat something fabulous in the gourmet restaurants of Paris. On two nights friends treated me. One night we had grilled pork chops au jus with golden roasted potatoes and glazed Belgian endive, the like of which I have never had since, and the second meal I can't quite remember because I was so intrigued with the company of my companion, but I think

*we had steak. I know we had Brie and an insidious
aperitif called Bhyrr.*

OMELETTE

There's nothing original about this but it's an easy meal for a
loner. I've never made an omelette that tasted as good as those
I had in Paris.

> **2 eggs**
> **2 teaspoons water**
> **Salt**
> **Pepper**
> **Pinch herbs (optional)**
> **1 tablespoon butter**
> **¼ cup grated cheese or ham**

Beat the eggs until light and foamy. Add the water, then sprinkle with salt, pepper, and herbs. In a skillet over medium heat,
melt the butter, tipping the pan to coat the bottom. Pour the egg
mixture into the pan. When the omelette is cooked but still moist
on top, sprinkle one-half with grated cheese or ham. Flip the
other half over to cover the cheese. Cook for a minute or two,
so cheese can melt. Slide omelette onto a serving plate. Heated
tomato soup as it comes from the can is a good sauce to pour over
an omelette.

OIYA BROTE
(Bread Omelette)

Egg bread or bread omelette that will help cover your bones.

> **½ loaf day-old bread**
> **½ cup butter (see what I mean?)**
> **3 eggs, beaten light**
> **½ cup milk**
> **Salt and pepper**

Cut the bread into cubes and brown them in the butter in a
frying pan. Beat the eggs, add milk and seasonings to taste; pour
them over the bread in the pan and fry until brown. Serve with
a sauce or a salad.

CHIVE BLOSSOM OMELETTE

A springtime treat that can be made when the chives are in bloom — or before and after.

> **4 eggs**
> **4 tablespoons milk or water**
> **½ teaspoon salt**
> **Pepper**
> **1 tablespoon finely chopped parsley**
> **1 teaspoon finely chopped chives**
> **2 tablespoons butter**
> **12 chive blossoms**

Beat the eggs just enough to blend the whites and yolks well. Add milk or water, seasoning, parsley, and chives. Melt the butter in a heavy pan and pour in the mixture. When the edges begin to set, reduce the heat. When the bottom is browned — watch it — sprinkle the blossoms over the omelette and fold it. Serve immediately on a heated plate. The blossoms add a delicious flavour and colour but the omelette without the blossoms can taste good at any time of the year.

SPANISH OMELETTE

Which I didn't have when I was in Spain.

> **1 tablespoon butter**
> **1 medium onion, finely sliced**
> **¼ cup chopped green pepper**
> **1 teaspoon flour**
> **1 tomato, cut up**
> **A few ripe or green olives, sliced**
> **Salt and pepper**
> **2 eggs, well beaten**

Melt the butter and cook the onion and green pepper until soft. Blend in the flour; stir in the tomato, olives, and seasonings. Cover and simmer, stirring occasionally while you cook the eggs. Pour the sauce over the cooked omelette or pour half on half the omelette, fold it over and pour the rest on top.

SCHNITZEL OIYAKUCHA
(Ham and Bacon Omelette)

A Mennonite omelette — very tasty.

¼ pound bacon, cut in pieces
¼ pound ham, chopped
4 onions, sliced
4 eggs, beaten slightly
4 tablespoons milk or cream
Salt and pepper

Fry the bacon until crisp; remove it from the pan and fry the ham in the bacon drippings until tender. Remove the ham and add it to the bacon. Fry the onions in some of the bacon drippings until soft and brown. Return the bacon and ham to the pan and mix with the onion. Beat the eggs and milk and seasonings together and pour them over the mixture in the pan. Cook slowly for 3 minutes. Serve on toast with a salad or sliced tomatoes.

FRENCH OR MENNONITE EGG TOAST

This is easier to make than pancakes, wonderful in an emergency or when you're alone and need nourishment. You can double, triple, or quintuple the recipe if your arithmetic is up to it.

1 egg, beaten
⅔ cup milk
Pinch salt
2 or 3 slices bread
Butter

Beat the egg, add the milk and salt and beat till they're blended. Soak the bread in the mixture, one piece at a time. Melt 2 teaspoons of butter in a frying pan and carefully slide the soaked bread into it. Fry, not too quickly, till it's brown on both sides and the centre is soft and set. You can use this with bacon, ketchup, relish, cheese, cold meat; some people sprinkle it with sugar and cinnamon, others spread it with jelly or jam; I pour lots of corn or maple syrup over mine.

FRENCH TOAST SANDWICHES

These hot sandwiches are ideal to serve at a luncheon with a green salad or sliced tomatoes. The sandwiches can be made ahead of time with any fillings you like: grated Cheddar, chopped ham, chopped chicken, tuna, chopped egg. You might use leftover sandwiches.

> **6 slices bacon, cut into bits**
> **1½ cups sandwich filling**
> **1 teaspoon grated onion (optional)**
> **¼ teaspoon dry mustard**
> **3 teaspoons cut-up parsley or celery**
> **3 tablespoons mayonnaise**
> **12 slices of bread, spread with butter**
> **2 eggs**
> **1 cup milk**
> **Salt and pepper**

Fry bacon bits until crisp, then drain on absorbent paper. With your sandwich filling, blend the onion, mustard, parsley, mayonnaise, and the bacon bits. Spread one side of the buttered bread thickly with the mixture and top with matching slice of bread — in other words, make a sandwich. Beat the eggs in a broad, shallow dish; mix in the milk, salt, and pepper. Dip the sandwiches in the mixture, first on one side, then the other, till they have absorbed some of the milk. Fry them in a little melted butter until golden brown on both sides. Serve hot.

CONNIE'S QUICKIE

This is super. Connie served it at a luncheon shower she had for me and I've been making it ever since.

Simply put thick slices of **tomato** on a piece of hot **buttered toast**. On each slice, put a half, or a quarter, of a hot **hard-boiled egg**. Sprinkle with **salt** and **pepper**, then cover with hot **cheese sauce** (page 88) and put strips of **fried bacon or crisp bacon bits** on top.

EGGS BENEDICT — WITH VARIATIONS

This is just a suggestion — great for a loner or for a special breakfast or a lunch with a green salad.

Make a **rich cream sauce or a cheese sauce** (page 88).

Fry as much **bacon** as you need, or sauté slices of **ham** and keep hot.

Split and toast as many **English muffins** as you need, or use toasted bread or buns.

Poach as many **eggs** as you need.

Now put them all together — the buttered, hot muffin on the bottom, next the bacon or ham, a slice of **tomato** if you have one, then the poached egg, and over all the rich creamy sauce. Sprinkle it with **paprika**, put a piece of **parsley** alongside and be grateful.

SCOTCH EGGS

When Norm and Ralph and I went to visit Kath in Devon, she drove us to Dartmouth, where we saw Scotch Eggs in the window of a delicatessen. We decided they'd be great to take on a picnic. And they were, with lettuce and salad dressing.

> **1 pound pork-sausage meat**
> **1 tablespoon — or less — prepared mustard**
> **Pepper**
> **6 hard-boiled eggs**
> **¾ cup dry fine breadcrumbs**
> **1 egg, beaten**
> **1 tablespoon water**
> **Chili sauce or lettuce and mayonnaise**

Combine the sausage meat, mustard, and pepper. Divide into 6 equal portions and wrap one portion around each shelled egg, coating egg completely. Roll it in breadcrumbs. Mix the raw egg and water. Dip each sausage-coated egg into the raw egg mixture. Roll again in the breadcrumbs. Place in a buttered shallow baking dish and bake at 400°F for about 30 minutes, or until browned, turning once during the baking. Cut into halves lengthwise; serve hot with chili sauce, or cold with lettuce and mayonnaise.

QUICK AND EASY

At a supermarket one day I decided to try some Canadian sardines; they were cheap, so I bought half a dozen cans. On opening a tin I found silver, soft-bellied fish of various sizes that I didn't like at all served on leaf lettuce as I do the neat, firm, more expensive little Norwegian sardines. What to do with six cans of home-grown fish? My thrifty, patriotic soul inspired me to invent this way of using them:

1 can sardines
2 tablespoons butter
2 tablespoons flour
1 teaspoon flavoured salt
1 cup milk
½ cup Cheddar cheese chunks (optional)
3 or 4 eggs
Thin slices of cheese
Salt
Sprinkle of cayenne pepper
2 tomatoes, sliced (optional)

Empty the sardines into a greased pie plate. With a knife slit the fish through the belly and easily remove the vertebral bones and anything else you see there that you don't like the look of. Spread the fish halves flat on the bottom of the pie plate and over them pour a medium-thick cream sauce made of the butter, flour, salt, and milk, with or without the cheddar chunks stirred into it. Break the eggs on top of the sauce, cover them with the slices of cheese and sprinkle with salt and cayenne. Put the dish into a 400°F oven and leave it there until the eggs are firm, then under the broiler (if necessary) till the cheese is bubbly. To make the dish look attractive, you might arrange a ring of tomato slices around the rim; if they are winter tomatoes, lay them on and bake them along with the rest. To serve, neatly slip sardines, sauce, egg, and tomato onto a piece of buttered toast on each plate.

This has been a great success; Canadian sardines are often on my shopping lists.

QUICKER AND EASIER

But not as good.

Pour undiluted **mushroom or tomato soup** into a pie plate; break **eggs** on top, spoon some soup over them, sprinkle with a mixture of **grated cheese** and **breadcrumbs** and put the pan into a 350°F oven till the eggs are firm, the soup bubbly, and the top is golden-brown. Serve on buttered toast or hot biscuits.

SARDINE-STUFFED EGGS

I discovered this to be another good way to use Canadian sardines. Cut **hard-boiled eggs** in half, remove the yolks. With a fork blend the yolks with **sardines**, a sprinkling of **cayenne**, **salt**, and enough **mayonnaise** to make the mixture creamy. Fill the egg whites with the mixture and garnish with parsley. Serve on lettuce with tomato slices, cucumbers, celery — and so forth.

SARDINE SALAD

Sometimes I mash half a can of **sardines** with **mayonnaise** and a spoonful of **ketchup**, stir in cut-up **celery** and finely sliced **lettuce**. I've never served it to visitors, but it gives me a good lunch.

MARDI'S EGG AND MUSHROOM LUNCHEON DISH

Mardi keeps telling me how great and simple this is; her mother used to make it.

> **Mushrooms**
> **Eggs**
> **Cream sauce (page 88)**
> **Toast or patty shells**

Sauté as many mushrooms as you think you might need (1 pound should be enough for 6 servings). Hard boil at least 1 egg per person. Make a cream sauce, using 2 cups of milk. Slice the eggs and stir them and the mushrooms into the cream sauce. Serve on buttered toast or in patty shells.

STUFFED EGGS IN JELLY

This is a jellied luncheon salad your guests will remember. It uses Canadian sardines.

> 2 tablespoons plain gelatine
> ½ cup cold water
> 3 cups well-seasoned chicken broth or broth made
>   with chicken-base powder or cubes
> ½ cup dry white wine
> 6 hard-boiled eggs
> 1 tin Canadian sardines, boned
> 3 tablespoons mayonnaise
> 2 teaspoons lemon juice
> Pepper and salt
> 2 sprigs parsley, finely cut

Soften the gelatine in cold water, dissolve in hot broth, add wine, and let cool. Cut the peeled eggs in half lengthwise and carefully remove yolks. Mash the egg yolks and sardines together, making a smooth paste with the mayonnaise, lemon juice, salt, pepper, and parsley. Fill the egg whites with the mixture and arrange the halves in a ring mould. (You may have some left for seconds in another mould or bowl.) Pour the gelatine mixture over the eggs, filling the mould. Chill until firm; then turn out on a plate with lettuce leaves, cucumber and zucchini slices, tomato wedges, bits of carrot, radish, celery, olives, or whatever, prettily arranged inside and around the ring. Pass mayonnaise, and if you've made hot cheese biscuits or buns you've got yourself a meal.

VARIATIONS

Instead of the Canadian sardines you might mince a few anchovies with the egg yolks. Or you might use grated blue cheese.

SPINACH SOUFFLÉ

One of Norm's favourite luncheon or supper dishes. Serve with a Greek salad, biscuits, or rolls.

2 packages spinach (fresh or frozen)
3 eggs, beaten
Salt and pepper
1 cup flour
1 cup grated Cheddar cheese
1 cup milk
½ cup butter
1 teaspoon baking powder

Cook the spinach, drain and chop a bit. Blend the beaten eggs, seasonings, flour, cheese, and milk; fold in the spinach. Melt the butter in an 8" x 12" cake pan and pour the spinach mixture into it. Bake at 350°F for about 45 minutes. Let sit for a few minutes to simmer down before cutting it in squares.

FISH DISHES

*Every Saturday morning, I go to the Waterloo Farmers'
Market to buy meat, fresh fruits, and vegetables from the
local farmers. I buy eggs and cream, strawberries and peas
from Hannah.*

*Once or twice a month I go to a supermarket. With a cart
I walk up and down the aisles, pausing at the little red
signs that mark the bargains. I may have only three or
four things on my shopping list, but I'll come up to the
check-out counter with my cart half filled.*

*Looking over my emergency cupboard, I always seem to
have too many tins of tuna, sardines, and canned tomato
and mushroom soup. Because of that constant surplus, I
keep looking for recipes that will use them. I have found
and used quite a few. Maybe you need them, too.*

SALMON OR TUNA CASSEROLE WITH BUTTERMILK BISCUITS

This is a complete meal and handsome enough for company. It's easy to cut in half if you want to serve only four.

> **2 tablespoons minced onion**
> **½ cup finely sliced celery**
> **3 tablespoons butter**
> **¼ cup flour**
> **2 cans salmon or tuna**
> **Milk**
> **¼ cup cream**
> **1 small can mushroom pieces, drained**
> **2 tablespoons snipped parsley**
> **Salt**
> **Sprinkle of cayenne pepper**
> **½ teaspoon thyme**
> **2 cups peas, canned, frozen, or fresh**
>
> *Biscuits:*
> **2 cups flour**
> **1 teaspoon baking soda**
> **1 teaspoon baking powder**
> **¼ teaspoon salt**
> **⅓ cup shortening**
> **⅔ cup buttermilk**

Sauté onion and celery in butter until onion is transparent; stir in ¼ cup flour. Drain the salmon and to the liquid add enough milk to make 1½ cups. Pour liquid over onion mixture, and stir until thickened. Add cream, mushrooms, parsley, salt, cayenne, and thyme, and mix well. Reserve ¼ cup peas for garnish; put the remaining peas in buttered casserole and pour salmon mixture over peas.

Now make the biscuits: sift flour, baking soda, baking powder, and salt together. Cut in the shortening until fine. Stir in the buttermilk. Turn the dough onto a floured board and roll ½ inch thick. Cut with small biscuit cutter and arrange biscuits around edge of casserole, putting the reserved peas in the centre. Bake at 425°F for 20 to 25 minutes till biscuits are golden.

TUNA PUFF CASSEROLE

Garnished with lemon slices and a sprig of green, this is a delight to behold — and to eat.

12 slices day-old bread
6 slices Cheddar cheese
2 cans tuna
⅔ cup mayonnaise
2 tablespoons minced onion
4 eggs, beaten
1½ cups milk
½ teaspoon mustard
¼ teaspoon Worcestershire sauce
½ teaspoon salt
Lemon slices

Arrange 6 of the bread slices in a shallow baking dish and cover with the cheese. Mix the tuna, mayonnaise, and onion and spread over the cheese slices. Cover with remaining 6 bread slices. Blend the eggs with the remaining ingredients. Pour gently over the bread. Refrigerate for one hour. Bake, uncovered, at 325°F for about 50 minutes, or until puffy and golden. Garnish with a lemon slice on each piece of bread and a bit of green.

RUBY'S FINNAN HADDIE CASSEROLE

Ruby's children always loved finnan haddie dinners.

1 piece finnan haddie, cooked and flaked
1 cup rice, cooked light and fluffy
½ cup hot milk
2 hard-boiled eggs, chopped
Lots of chopped parsley
2 tablespoons melted butter
Salt and pepper

Topping:
½ cup breadcrumbs
¼ cup grated cheese

Mix all together in a buttered casserole and sprinkle the breadcrumbs mixed with the cheese on top. Bake in a 350°F oven till hot and nicely toasted.

SHRIMP CASSEROLE

Norm often makes this mild, delicious dish when she has people in for a buffet supper; it always goes over well with a tossed salad, vegetable, and relishes.

¼ cup chopped onion
2 tablespoons butter
2 tablespoons flour
2 cups milk, heated
½ teaspoon Worcestershire sauce (optional)
½ teaspoon celery salt
½ teaspoon ordinary salt
Dash pepper and cayenne
2 cups fresh or canned sliced mushrooms
2 cups cleaned, cooked shrimp
2 cups cooked rice
½ cup shredded sharp cheese
½ cup buttered bread or cracker crumbs

Cook the onion in butter until tender but not brown. Make a thin cream sauce by blending the flour with the butter and onion, pouring in the milk and stirring till slightly thickened; blend in the seasonings, and add the mushrooms, cooked first in butter. Stir in the cooked shrimp and the cooked rice. Pour into a casserole, top with a mixture of cheese and buttered crumbs. Bake in a 350°F oven for 20 to 30 minutes.

SALMON OR TUNA WRAP-UP

This will help the salmon or tuna go a bit farther.

>2 tablespoons butter
>1 onion, finely chopped
>1 cup chopped celery
>2 tins salmon or tuna, drained
>Salt and pepper
>1 egg, slightly beaten
>
>*Biscuit dough:*
>¼ cup butter or margarine
>2 cups flour
>3 teaspoons baking powder
>¼ teaspoon salt
>¾ cup milk

In the 2 tablespoons of butter, sauté the onion and celery till the onion is soft; mix it with the fish, adding seasonings to taste; stir in the beaten egg. Make biscuit dough. Cut the butter into the dry ingredients, add the milk. Roll into an oblong about ½ inch thick. Line a loaf pan with the dough, pour in the fish mixture and tuck the dough over it, leaving a vent down the centre. Or spread the fish mixture over the oblong of dough, roll it up like a jelly roll, and drop it into a loaf pan. Bake for about 15 minutes in a 400°F oven; keep your eye on it.

Serve with plenty of white sauce (page 88) generously flavoured with chopped parsley, or herbs and chopped hard-boiled eggs. And a green salad.

TUNA ROLL

>2 cans tuna, drained
>1 egg, slightly beaten
>½ cup chopped onion
>½ cup grated cheese
>½ cup chopped parsley
>1 teaspoon celery salt
>Pepper
>1 cup peas or corn

Biscuit dough:
2 cups flour
½ teaspoon salt
1 tablespoon baking powder
½ cup milk

Mix the tuna, egg, onion, cheese, parsley, celery salt, pepper, and peas. To make dough, mix the flour, salt, baking powder, and milk. On a floured surface, roll dough into a 15" x 10" rectangle. Spread with tuna mixture. Roll like a jelly roll, beginning at the long side. Seal the edges. Place sealed-side down on a buttered baking sheet. Slash top of roll with a knife. Bake at 375°F for 25 to 30 minutes, or until brown. Serve with cheese or parsley sauce (page 88).

SALMON PATTIES

Mother often made salmon patties because they were quick and easy and we loved them. Daddy liked patties with chili sauce. Mother liked ketchup. We kids liked them plain.

1 large can salmon
1 egg, slightly beaten
2 tablespoons finely grated onion
2 tablespoons flour
2 tablespoons lemon juice
¼ teaspoon salt
Pepper
2 tablespoons chopped parsley
1 teaspoon Worcestershire sauce
1 cup cold mashed potatoes
¼ cup breadcrumbs
3 tablespoons butter

In a large bowl, flake the salmon and liquid with a fork. Add remaining ingredients except breadcrumbs and butter. Mix until blended. Shape into 9 patties, using about ¼ cup of the mixture for each. (You could make more smaller ones.) Flatten each patty slightly, then dip into breadcrumbs to coat. In a large pan over medium heat, melt the butter and brown both sides of patties. Garnish with parsley.

TUNABURGERS

Great for a quick lunch — or even for your bridge club.

1 can tuna
2 tablespoons chopped onion
1 cup grated Cheddar cheese
4 hard-boiled eggs, chopped
½ cup mayonnaise
2 tablespoons chopped celery
8 hamburger buns

Combine tuna, onion, cheese, egg, mayonnaise, and celery; mix well. Open the buns; spoon mixture on one half. Cover with other half and wrap each in foil. Cook at 250°F for about 30 minutes, or until hot.

PUFFY TUNA SANDWICHES

Good, good.

1 can tuna (or salmon, crabmeat, or shrimp)
1½ teaspoons mustard
¼ teaspoon Worcestershire sauce
¼ cup mayonnaise
1½ teaspoons grated onion
2 tablespoons chopped green pepper or celery
3 hamburger buns, split in half
6 slices tomato
½ cup grated Cheddar cheese

Mix tuna, mustard, Worcestershire sauce, ¼ cup of the mayonnaise, onion, and green pepper. Spoon onto buns. Top each with a tomato slice. Blend remaining ½ cup mayonnaise with cheese, then spread on tomato slices. Place the buns on a cookie sheet, set 4 inches from heat, and broil until topping puffs and browns, about 5 minutes.

FOR LONERS AND COUPLES

You'll eat a lot better if you have a little broil, bake, and toast oven that stands on your kitchen counter. Often you wouldn't bother to heat up your big oven to bake one serving of chicken and a potato, but if you have a small oven you'll find yourself able to cook all sorts of things in small quantities so much more quickly and just as effectively as you would in a big one.

The oven heats up almost instantly; you can bake a potato in half to three-quarters of an hour, as well as a piece of chicken. You can make a meat loaf, broil chops, steak, cutlets. You can even make half a dozen muffins. You can bake a soufflé, a casserole, reheat buns, biscuits, and vegetables. You can make toast. If you have one, you'll think of all sorts of ways to use it. When I finally got mine I wondered why I had waited so long.

Two years ago I had wiring put into my kitchen for a microwave oven; maybe some day I'll buy one. I keep hearing they're useful and sometimes I'm tempted, but I never seem to have time to go shopping.

SINGLE SUPPER

Last night I thought I was making enough of this for two meals, but it was so good I ate all of it at one.

1 large tomato, frozen or fresh
Butter
2 slices of whole-wheat bread
Cheddar cheese, sliced
1 or 2 eggs
Salt and pepper
¼ teaspoon mixed dried herbs

I put a large tomato in a pie plate and stuck it under the grill while I buttered the bread which I then put under the tomato, cut in half, to sop up the juices. Next I sliced enough Cheddar to cover the bread and tomatoes completely and put that under the grill till it bubbled. Then I broke an egg into the middle of the dish, sprinkled it with salt, pepper, and herbs. I pricked the yolk so it ran over the tomato and cheese, and put it under the grill again — in my little toast 'n broil oven — till the egg became solid, but not tough. If I'd had a slice or two of bacon, I would have grilled that on top of the egg at the same time. But you can't have everything.

KIT'S HAMBURGER WITH A FRENCH ACCENT FOR TWO

Kit often has to get a meal in a hurry when she comes home from the Brantford *Expositer*.

2 ground beef patties
Flour
1 teaspoon butter
1 bouillon cube
4 tablespoons water
4 tablespoons red wine

Dredge the patties in flour; melt the butter in a skillet and cook the patties to the doneness you prefer. (Patties cook more quickly if a hole is poked in the centre after shaping.) Place in the oven at 100°F to keep warm. Drain the excess fat from the skillet, but keep all the brown bits. Place bouillon cube and water in skillet, and stir over low heat, as you scrape the pan with a wooden spoon, until the bouillon has dissolved. Add red wine and stir a minute or two. Spoon the sauce over the patties. (You might add sliced mushrooms to the skillet, and cook them a few minutes before proceeding with the bouillon cube.) Kit serves this with French bread and a tossed salad.

When my French friend Françoise came to Canada for the first time, she was excited when we made hamburgers on the barbecue near the lake. She said, "I am new born; I have had my first hamburger."

SPINACH SOUFFLÉ FOR TWO

For two? I ate all of this at one sitting.

> **About ⅓ package raw spinach**
> **½ small onion, cut up**
> **½ cup milk**
> **¼ cup Cheddar cheese**
> **2 eggs, separated**
> **2 tablespoons butter**
> **2 tablespoons flour**
> **Salt and pepper**

Cut the raw spinach leaves coarsely and drop them into your blender or food processor with all the rest of the ingredients but the egg whites. Blend until the spinach and onion are evenly fine. Pour all into a saucepan and stir over medium heat until thickened. Let it cool slightly. Beat the egg whites till stiff, then fold them into the spinach mixture and turn it into a buttered oven dish. Bake in a 325°F oven for 30 to 40 minutes, till it is firm when you insert a knife. It will puff up impressively and have real flavour when you serve it alone or with a mushroom or tomato sauce and toast or English muffins.

SARDINE CRISPIES

You might not believe it till you try it but **sardines** dipped in **egg** and **dried bread or cracker crumbs** then sautéed in **oil and butter** are so crisp and good that you'll want to eat them quite often.

I buy the tiny imported expensive sardines to eat as they are with lettuce; I also buy cans of the sardines packed in New Brunswick to use when I make something that combines them or cooks them. I thought one can would be enough for two meals of Sardine Crispies but I enjoyed them so much that I ate the whole lot with a green salad and the leftover egg in which the sardines were dipped, poured into the pan after the fish were crisp and golden. There wasn't any left for my cats, Willie and Cicely.

Simplicity

Simplicity, economy, and experience are the keynotes of Mennonite cooking. Recipes are invented to make use of everything that is grown on Waterloo County farms. Fruits are canned, pickled, or made into juicy pies. Beef and ham are cured with maple smoke; pork scraps become well-seasoned sausages. Sour milk is made into cheeses; sour cream is used in salads and cakes.

LEVAVASCHT MIT BUNS
(Headcheese Burgers)

Very quick and tasty.

Split **hamburger rolls** and on each half tailor to fit a slice of **headcheese or liverwurst**; slip under the broiler and brown it or let it become bubbly. **Relish or slices of onion and tomato**, raw or broiled, on top gives you a lunch.

ANOTHER EASY ONE

To use up those miserable winter tomatoes.

Butter a custard cup, put half a **tomato** in the bottom, break an **egg** over it, sprinkle it with **salt** and **pepper**, then about half an inch of **cheese** cubes mixed with **breadcrumbs**. Put it in the oven till the egg is firm. Serve on buttered or grilled cheese toast.

ANOTHER VERSION

I put a frozen **tomato** into my toaster oven until it is soft and there is liquid all around it; into the liquid I drop enough **herbed croutons or prepared bread stuffing** to sop it up. I break an **egg** over the tomato and sprinkle the whole thing with **grated Cheddar or Parmesan cheese**. Under the broiler the egg cooks fairly quickly and I have a nourishing meal.

LEFTOVER MEAT DISHES

In Bevvy's and my houses, nothing is wasted. Leftover meats are jellied, pickled, warmed over, or combined with vegetables and noodles to make nourishing suppers. From Bevvy I have learned that hot gravy is delicious on bread; beef dripping makes the best-flavoured shortening for frying potatoes, onions, wieners, or steaks; chicken fat, pure and mild, gives cookies a delicate crispness; bacon dripping is the preferred base for warm sour-cream salads.

"And goose grease we use for rubbing on sore throats and chests when the children have colds," Bevvy tells me. "Or for water-proofing their boots. And whatever fat we have that we can't use any other way yet, we pour in a kettle with lye and make soap."

PAHNHAAS OR SCRAPPLE

"Pahnhaas" means pan rabbit, though there is no rabbit in it. This is a popular old-timer. Mother ate hers with maple syrup poured over it but Bevvy serves it with relish or a salad. Mother bought liver sausage, ate what she wanted of it and used the rest for Pahnhaas — at least two inches of sausage with 2 cupfuls of cornmeal. Pahnhaas can be made with ground meat or head cheese as well.

> **2 cups cornmeal**
> **4 to 6 cups boiling water (enough to make a stiff porridge with the cornmeal)**
> **1 teaspoon salt**
> **A piece of liverwurst**

Mother boiled the cornmeal, water, and salt in a big kettle because it spurts up when it's boiling and she didn't want it to spatter her stove. She added the liver sausage which melted as it was stirred into the porridge and kept stirring till the mixture was thick enough to drop off the spoon in a lump and she could hardly stir it any more. She then pressed it into a greased loaf pan and let it cool. Next day she'd slice it ⅛ of an inch thick and fry it in shortening till it was crisp and deliciously brown on both sides.

FRIED CORNMEAL MUSH

Bevvy often makes cornmeal porridge in exactly the same way as Pahnhaas but without the meat; she fries and serves it with maple syrup or apple butter, not because it is economical but because it is good.

FRIED OATMEAL PORRIDGE

Thick oatmeal porridge pressed into a loaf pan to set, then cut into pancake-thin slices and fried is another Mennonite favourite. "Till you've had it served with lots of fresh maple syrup," Bevvy says, "you don't know what a real treat you have missed."

LEFTOVER ROAST

If you have quite a lot of the roast left over after dinner, put it into an earthenware pot or casserole with a heavy, tight lid; pour the gravy over it and the leftover onions that went with the roast; you might put in carrots and any other mild vegetables too. Refrigerate. Next day, or a couple of days after, pop the pot into a 325°F oven for not quite an hour — it just needs to be there long enough to be thoroughly heated. Because the pot is tightly covered, the meal will have no leftover meat flavour; it will be like a delicious pot-roast — which is what it may have been in the first place.

LEFTOVER CHICKEN OR TURKEY LOAF

This is a good way to finish up the bird. If you have bread dressing left over, you could blend it in too. If you have lots of it, you could simply mix it with the chopped meat, stir in some gravy, and pack it into a loaf pan to bake.

> **6 cups finely chopped, cooked chicken or turkey**
> **1 cup mayonnaise**
> **½ cup breadcrumbs**
> **½ cup chopped green pepper**
> **½ cup chopped onion**
> **½ cup chili sauce**
> **1 teaspoon salt**
> **Pepper**

Combine all ingredients in a bowl and mix well. Press into a buttered loaf pan and bake at 350°F for 30 minutes or until lightly browned. Serve with cream, cheese, or mushroom soup.

LEFTOVER CHICKEN DISH

Whenever I have a roast chicken dinner, I always hope there'll be enough of everything left over to make this delicious dish the next day. Into a well-greased oven dish cut up into bite-size pieces the **chicken** — and **dressing**, if there is some. With it, mix plenty of leftover **gravy** or make a sauce by blending **milk**,

chicken soup or bouillon powder, and **flour** — it will thicken as it cooks. Over the chicken mixture spread your leftover **vegetables** — or canned ones. Remash your leftover **potatoes** with plenty of **butter** and **cream or milk** and spread smoothly over the top and dot with **butter**. Cover the dish and bake it at 350°F or thereabouts, for about 45 minutes; remove the lid and let the potatoes brown a bit before serving. With a green salad and leftover cranberries you'll have a wonderful meal.

CHICKEN, BEEF, OR TURKEY CURRY

If you like curry, you'll like this. It certainly peps up the left-overs.

¼ **cup butter**
¼ **cup chopped onion**
¼ **cup flour**
1 **teaspoon salt**
½ **teaspoon ginger**
1 **tablespoon curry powder**
2 **cups milk**
2 **cups diced cooked meat**
¼ **cup chopped celery**
1 **cup chopped apple**
2 **cups hot cooked rice**
½ **cup toasted slivered almonds or sunflower seeds**
Crumbled crisp bacon

Melt butter, add onion and sauté for 5 minutes. Blend in flour and seasonings. Gradually add milk, stirring constantly till thickened. Add turkey or whatever meat you use, celery, and apple; cook for 5 minutes longer. Serve over a bed of rice, sprinkling almonds and bacon on top. Serve with a green salad.

LEFTOVER TURKEY CASSEROLE

Save some of your Christmas dinner to make this good-tasting dish.

> **3 cups diced cooked turkey (more or less)**
> **1 cup mayonnaise**
> **1 cup grated Cheddar cheese**
> **1 cup chopped celery**
> **1 onion, chopped**
> **1 green pepper, chopped**
> **½ cup slivered almonds or sunflower seeds**
> **Salt**
> **Crushed potato chips or buttered breadcrumbs**

Combine all the ingredients; mix well. Place in a casserole and bake at 350°F for 45 minutes or until the vegetables are soft, or for 35 minutes if you like them to stay crisp. During the last 10 minutes of baking you might like to sprinkle the top with potato chips or buttered breadcrumbs.

PORK PIE

One of the best ways to use leftover pork.

> **2½ cups, more or less, cold roast pork cut in cubes**
> **2 medium-tart apples, cored and sliced**
> **1 cup, more or less, leftover gravy**
> **Pastry to cover**
> **Salt and pepper**

Grease a shallow baking dish and put into it alternate layers of pork and apples. Season each layer with salt and pepper. Pour the gravy over all and cover the dish with pastry. Prick or slash the crust to let steam out during baking. Put in a 400°F oven until the crust starts to brown; reduce heat to 350°F and bake another half hour.

BYE-BYE SHORTCAKE

This is a tasty way to use up leftover chicken or turkey — and fancy too.

Biscuit dough:
2 cups flour
4 teaspoons baking powder
½ teaspoon salt
⅓ cup shortening
⅔ cup milk

Blend the ingredients in the order given. Roll out the dough on a board to ½-inch thickness; cut out rounds with a drinking glass; then cut a round hole in half the rounds — like a doughnut. Brush whole rounds with melted shortening, place doughnut-shaped pieces on top and bake in a 450°F oven for 15 minutes.
   While the biscuits are baking make the meat sauce:

2 tablespoons butter
6 tablespoons flour
Salt and pepper
2 cups milk or milk and gravy
2 cups cooked cubed meat
2 tablespoons cut up parsley
Cranberry sauce or jelly

Melt the butter; add the flour, salt, pepper, and slowly the milk and gravy; stir till it thickens. Add the meat and parsley. When the biscuits are baked, deftly separate the doughnut-shaped biscuits from the whole rounds. Pour meat sauce over the lower half of the biscuit, put biscuit ring on top and put a spoonful of cranberry sauce or jelly in the hole as a garnish. Add a salad and you have a good meal.

HANDY COTTAGE PIE

For those last bits of meat that nobody wants cold.

> **2 tablespoons butter**
> **2 cups diced cooked meat — beef, pork, veal,
>   lamb, or fowl**
> **3 tablespoons flour**
> **1 can vegetable soup diluted to make 2 cups**
> **Parsley or herbs**
> **Mashed potatoes and gravy, if there is any leftover**

Melt the butter, add the diced meat and cook until lightly browned. Add the flour and stir until well blended. Gradually add leftover gravy and the vegetable soup; cook, stirring constantly until the mixture thickens. You might add some parsley or herbs if you like. Turn into a baking dish and cover the top thickly and roughly with fluffy mashed potatoes. Bake in a 375°F oven for about 15 minutes until nicely browned.

HOT HAM ROLLS

Tired of eating leftover ham? Let it come to this glorious end.

> *Filling:*
> **2 tablespoons butter**
> **2 tablespoons flour**
> **1 cup milk**
> **2 cups ground ham**

> *Dough:*
> **2 cups flour**
> **1 tablespoon baking powder**
> **½ teaspoon salt**
> **¼ cup vegetable shortening**
> **¾ cup milk**

> **2 tablespoons chopped parsley**

In a saucepan over medium heat, melt the butter and blend in flour. Gradually stir in the milk until the mixture thickens. Set aside about ¼ cup for the topping. Stir in the ham.

To make the dough, sift flour, baking powder, and salt together; cut in shortening until crumbly. Add milk and mix until dough clings. Roll out the dough into a rectangle ⅛-inch thick.

Spread the ham mixture over it and roll up like a jelly roll. Cut into one-inch slices; place cut-side-up on greased baking pan. Bake at 400°F for 25 minutes or until rolls are browned. Heat the remaining white sauce. Pour over top and sprinkle with parsley. Serve hot, with a salad and pickled beets.

NOODLES AND HAM

There's nothing unusual about this but it tastes good.

> **2 cups noodles, cooked**
> **2 cups cooked ham, chopped**
> **2 cups thin white sauce (page 88)**
> **⅔ cup grated cheese**

Put a layer of noodles in a greased oven dish. Add a layer of ham, cover with well-seasoned white sauce, and sprinkle with cheese. Repeat layers of noodles, ham and white sauce until all the ingredients are used. Sprinkle cheese on top — mixed with a few breadcrumbs. Bake in a 350°F oven for 30 minutes.

LEFTOVER HAM CASSEROLE

My mother never made leftover concoctions; maybe because no one suggested a way to do it. This way could be varied to use whatever you have left over.

> **1 or 2 cups leftover ham or beef**
> **Cabbage, sliced**
> **1 or 2 onions, sliced**
> **Several carrots, cut in pieces**
> **Several potatoes, peeled and quartered**
> **1 or 2 stalks celery, sliced**
> **½ cup water**
> **1 bay leaf**
> **Salt**

Put everything into a heavy pot and simmer until the potatoes are soft.

HAM LOAF

You'll be proud of this. It can be served hot or cold.

> 3 tablespoons butter
> 5 tablespoons brown sugar
> 3 slices pineapple
> 1½ pounds cooked, ground ham
> 2 eggs, lightly beaten
> ½ cup breadcrumbs
> ¼ cup milk
> Pepper

Melt the butter in the loaf pan in which you are going to bake the loaf, add the sugar, stir until it is blended, then put in the pieces of pineapple which should cover the bottom of the pan. Mix the ham and eggs, add the crumbs, milk and pepper; spread on top of the sugar and pineapple and bake in a 350° to 400°F oven for about an hour.

HAM AND PEAS ON TOAST OR ENGLISH MUFFINS

A quick supper for a family or a loner.

> 2 tablespoons butter
> 2 tablespoons flour
> 1 cup milk
> 1 cup grated cheese
> 1 can peas
> 2 cups chopped ham
> 2 hard-boiled eggs, chopped
> Toast or English muffins

Melt butter and stir in flour. Slowly add milk and cook until thick, stirring constantly. Add remaining ingredients, except toast, stirring carefully; cook until heated through. Serve over buttered toast or toasted English muffins.

KARTOFFELKRAPFEN
(Potato Meat Cakes)

Another wonderful way of using up leftover potatoes and leftover meat as well.

>   4 cups mashed potatoes
>   1 cup flour
>   2 teaspoons baking powder
>   3 eggs
>   3 cups chopped leftover meat
>   3 tablespoons ketchup, mushroom sauce, or gravy
>   Cut-up chives and parsley
>   Salt and pepper
>   Fine breadcrumbs
>   ¼ cup butter

Blend the potatoes, flour sifted with baking powder, and 2
beaten eggs. Roll to almost ½-inch thickness on a well-floured
board. Cut into rounds about 5 inches across. Put a large dollop
of the meat mixed with the ketchup, chives, and seasonings in
the centre of each. Fold and press the edges firmly together.
Brush with the third beaten egg and dip in breadcrumbs. Melt
butter in baking pan. Put cakes in pan and bake in a 400°F oven
until a golden brown. A fish filling made with a thick cream
sauce may be used instead of meat.

STUFFED SQUASH

You could use leftover squash as well as leftover meat with this.

3 pepper squash
2 tablespoons melted butter
Salt and pepper
1 cup cooked meat
2½ cups soft breadcrumbs
Minced onion — much or little
2 tablespoons ketchup
Dash Worcestershire sauce
Soup stock or water or broth to moisten

Wipe the squash and cut in half lengthwise. Remove the seeds and stringy portion, then place a little butter in the hollowed halves and sprinkle with salt and pepper. Cover and bake in a 450°F oven for 30 to 45 minutes until almost tender. Mix up the remaining ingredients and fill up the squash. Return to the oven for about 15 minutes and serve hot, hot, hot.

GEROLT FLAISCH
(Meat Roll)

Biscuit dough:
2 cups flour
4 teaspoons baking powder
½ teaspoon salt
5 tablespoons shortening
⅔ cup milk

Meat filling:
1½ cups chopped cooked meat — or more
2 tablespoons minced onion
5 tablespoons gravy
Seasonings

Mix the biscuit dough ingredients in the order given and roll ¼-inch thick. Spread with the meat filling. Roll up like a jelly roll and cut in slices 1 inch thick. Place pieces in a buttered baking pan. Dot with butter, bake in 450°F oven about 15 minutes. Serve with additional gravy poured over it — or one of your own ingenious sauces — like mushroom or tomato soup.

LEFTOVER SUPPER

When Harold Horwood was writer-in-residence at the University of Waterloo, he often came out to Sunfish for supper. While he sat in my swivel chair and read a book or a magazine, I puttered in the kitchen — often with leftovers from Sunday's company dinner. One night there was a fair chunk of leftover pork roast (it could have been beef, chicken, turkey, or what have you).

1 cup leftover gravy (more or less)
1 cup water
5 or 6 old winter carrots, grated (easy in my food processor)
1 onion, finely chopped (food processor again)
2 potatoes, finely sliced (leftover or raw)
Leftover meat, sliced or cut into bite-size pieces
2 pinches thyme
2 tablespoons finely chopped parsley (fresh or frozen)
Tea biscuits

I boiled the gravy, water, carrots, onion, and potatoes until they looked mushy, almost like a sauce. Then I added the rest of the ingredients and put the mixture in a square pyrex pan. I dug out some tea biscuits from my freezer (I could have mixed up the dough for Bye-Bye Shortcake, page 75), put the biscuits on top, put the pan into a 350°F oven until the whole lot was bubbling and the biscuits were thawed (or baked if I'd started from scratch). Along with this I heated some leftover squash. And Harold and I ate every bit — with pickled beets and a raw cabbage salad.

LEFTOVER MEAT CASSEROLE

A good follow-up after a Sunday dinner — with many variations.

> **2 cups cubed cooked meat**
> **1 cup diced celery**
> **An onion or two that went with your roast**
> **1 cup leftover vegetables**
> **3 cups cooked noodles**
> **1 can tomato soup**
> **1 can mushroom soup**
> **1 teaspoon salt**
> **Pepper**
> **1 cup meat broth or gravy**
> **½ cup grated Cheddar cheese**
> **1 cup breadcrumbs**

Combine the meat and vegetables. Arrange mixture in a casserole with noodles in alternate layers — with noodles on top.
Blend the soups, seasonings, and the gravy and pour into the
casserole. Sprinkle grated cheese mixed with breadcrumbs over
the top and bake in a 350°F oven for an hour or so. It's good
enough for company.

OLD STANDBY

There always comes a time — in my life, anyway — when I resort to this: made of leftover or fresh vegetables and ground meat, it's often surprisingly good.

No list of ingredients: I simply open my fridge and see what is in there that ought to come out. Then I supplement. In the bottom of a casserole I slice **potatoes** — raw or cooked ones — then a layer of whatever **vegetables** I have found: carrots, beans, peas, peppers, corn, parsnips, asparagus, even cabbage, broccoli, cauliflower, sprouts. The layer may be as thick as you like, but don't overdo it. If I want to use **ground meat** I fry it with sliced **onion** until it is slightly browned and spread it over the vegetables. If I use leftover meat I sauté the onion and mix it with the meat and leftover **gravy**. Finally, to give the dish the moisture it needs, I put enough **tomatoes** on top (raw, canned, or frozen ones cut in quarters). I forgot to mention: **salt, pepper**, and sprinkle with **herbs** each layer as you put it in. Cover the dish, put it in a 325°F oven for an hour or so and enjoy the illusion of a great meal coming up, because it will really smell good and often that's half the battle, isn't it? Or is it? Taste it and see. As long as there are no bones in the dish you can always scrape it into your blender and whizz it into an incredible soup.

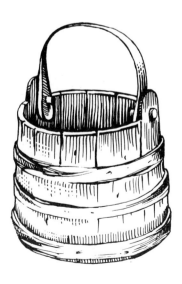

HAROLD HORWOOD'S CHINESE DISHES

Harold is a very special person: Newfoundland's award-winning novelist, naturalist, journalist, politician, teacher, explorer, he also does most of the cooking for his Bay of Fundy household which is frequently expanded to more than fourteen because Harold takes in many strays and visiting writers. He learned about cooking in a Chinese restaurant.

While he was writer-in-residence at the University of Western Ontario, Harold came to my house one day with his wife Corky, little Andrew, baby Leah, and all the makings for a Chinese meal. He prepared it, we greatly enjoyed it, and he sent me his recipes for my cookbook. He wrote:

"Though the main part of the Chinese cuisine is an acquired skill that cannot be taught from recipes, Clear and Egg Drop Soup, Foo Yong (omelette), and barbecued meats can be done successfully by anybody."

All Harold's recipes use Chinese soy sauce. He says American or Japanese soy sauces are double in strength. If you use American sauce reduce to half the amount and add water to make up. Japanese soy sauce should be avoided altogether because it is not only double strength but also nearly saturated with salt.

CHINESE CLEAR SOUP

2 cups stock (beef, chicken, pork, or shellfish)
1 tablespoon Chinese soy sauce
3 or 4 medium-sized mushrooms, thinly sliced
1 cup thin egg noodles
1 small green onion with leaves, sliced
¼ cup bean sprouts (optional)

To boiling stock, add soy sauce and mushroom slices; boil for 3 minutes. Drop in the noodles and boil 3 minutes longer. Just before removing from the heat add sliced onion and bean sprouts.

EGG DROP SOUP

2 cups Clear Soup (above)
1 egg

While the soup comes to a boil, beat an egg with a fork until it is fairly thin; when the soup boils vigorously, pour the egg into it from a height of 2 feet or so, stirring the soup as you do it. Remove from heat at once and serve.

BARBECUE SAUCE

Harold writes: "You begin by making the sauce."

¼ **cup molasses**
½ **cup Chinese soy sauce**
½ **cup water**
2 **teaspoons powdered ginger**
½ **teaspoon powdered cloves**
½ **teaspoon powdered onion**
¼ **teaspoon powdered garlic**

Put everything in a large screw-capped jar and shake it up. That's all. Shake it again before using it, as the spices may tend to settle. To make Garlic Sauce for garlic ribs, you simply add more garlic.

CHICKEN AND TURKEYS

Harold roasts **fowl** in a covered pan with **barbecue sauce** poured generously over them, inside and out, basting them frequently, till they are brown and tender.

BARBECUED CUBED PORK OR BARBECUED SPARE RIBS

Start cooking **cubed pork or spare ribs** in hot **oil** in a wok or a large frying pan. (The wok is no advantage except for a mixed dish that requires various cooking times.) After three or four minutes of stirring the meat with a spatula, pour in the **barbecue sauce** (above) in a reasonable quantity and keep stirring over high heat until the sauce disappears and the meat is tender.

FOO YONG

Harold says this amount makes a refreshingly different breakfast or lunch for two.

3 eggs
1 teaspoon Chinese soy sauce
½ to 1 cup fresh sliced mushrooms or bean sprouts
2 tablespoons vegetable oil

Harold directs: Start by pre-heating one of the large elements on the surface of your stove until it is red, and the top element of your oven until it's good and bloody hot. In a bowl, beat the eggs with a fork until they reach the classic omelette stage; stir in the soy sauce until the colour is more or less even. Heat the oil in a large frying pan until it begins to smoke. Pour in the egg mixture and immediately remove from the heat. Over the surface of the uncooked egg, sprinkle generously the mushroom slices or bean sprouts. Put the pan in the oven 6 inches beneath the heated top element; peek every few seconds to see when the eggs begin to bubble then take the pan out and fold the egg over like an omelette.

Harold says, "I recommend that you try not more than three eggs at a time. If you have to cook for a crowd, do the three-egg thing over and over again. Each panful takes only about two minutes."

SAUCES

WHITE (OR CREAM) SAUCE

2 tablespoons butter
2 tablespoons flour
1 cup milk
Salt and pepper

Melt the butter, add the flour, and stir until blended. Slowly add the milk and cook until the mixture thickens, stirring constantly. Add seasonings.

CHEESE SAUCE

Make a white sauce and in it melt ¼ to ½ **cup cut-up or grated cheese**. Stir till smooth.

MUSHROOM SAUCE

2 tablespoons butter
½ cup finely sliced mushrooms
2 tablespoons flour
1 cup milk
Salt and pepper

Melt the butter, add the mushrooms and stir in the butter over medium heat for about 5 minutes — till the mushrooms are cooked. Blend in the flour, slowly add the milk, and stir until the mixture thickens. If doing all this is too much trouble, simply open a can of mushroom soup and use it as mushroom sauce where required.

PARSLEY SAUCE

Put lots of **very finely cut-up fresh parsley** in white sauce.

LOW-CALORIE CHEESE SAUCE

This is a quick and easy one and almost as good as something richer.

> **2 cups water**
> **3 tablespoons flour**
> **4 tablespoons instant milk powder (or more)**
> **1 teaspoon flavoured salt**
> **⅛ teaspoon pepper**
> **1 or 2 tablespoons very sharp, grated Cheddar cheese (or more)**

Put the water in your blender. Measure in all the rest except the cheese and blend till it's foamy. Pour into a heavy saucepan at high heat, stirring all the time. It thickens in a few minutes. Take it off the stove, add the grated cheese and stir till it melts. That's it. If you want a thicker sauce add more flour. Use it without the cheese as a cream sauce. Or put in herbs or any other flavouring you like; the calorie count will stay down. Basic cream sauces can be flavoured with dill, curry powder, pimiento.

TOMATO CREAM SAUCE

So easy and so zestful — to put over an omelette or soufflé or anything that needs a delicious sauce.

Some **cream of tomato soup** (undiluted from a can) mixed with some **sour cream**. Try it and you'll see. Taste till you think it's just right to suit you.

INDEX